MIMESIS
INTERNATIONAL

PHILOSOPHY

n. 67

Federico Bina

HARD-WIRED PSYCHOLOGY AND MORAL CHANGE

The publication of this volume has been partly funded by the European Union through the National Recovery and Resilience Plan (NRRP)—Mission 4, Component 2, Investment 1.1—"Fund for the National Research Program and for Projects of National Interest (NRP)", under grant agreement P2022RBTX4 "Distrust in Science Reframed: Understanding and Countering Anti-scientific Behavior" (CUP D53D23019800001). The information and opinions are those of the author and do not necessarily reflect the opinion of the European Commission.

Isbn: 9788869774843
Book series: *Philosophy,* n. 67

CONTENTS

To my grandmother Pinu,
and in memory of my grandfather Titta,
the most beautiful, extraordinary, and unexpected
examples of moral change I have witnessed

INTRODUCTION

This book discusses and criticizes the idea that human psychology
and morality are direct products of evolution by natural selection,
and that this would significantly influence both the psychology and
content of moral beliefs and norms, constituting a major obstacle to
significant psychological, epistemic, and moral change (Sauer 2019;
2023; Persson & Savulescu 2012; 2017; Klenk & Sauer 2020; Street
2006; Levy 2021). In the recent scientific and philosophical debate,
many scholars have defended this view on the basis of adaptationist
and functionalist hypotheses about the natural evolution of moral
cognition and institutions (Joyce 2006; Tomasello 2016; Guardo
2024). These views state that selective pressures in small and close-
knit pre-modern societies, in which humanity has lived for most of
its evolutionary history, favored a tribalistic, exclusive, and short-
sighted psychology, which continues to strongly influence and limit
human cognition and behavior nowadays, as decades of experimental
research in cognitive, social and moral psychology would confirm.
This cognitive architecture is seen by many as very hard, if not
impossible, to modify; and the same would be true for moral beliefs
and cultures that inevitably depend on evaluative attitudes that are
directly shaped by selective pressures (Street 2006; Joyce 2006;
Persson & Savulescu 2017).
This work investigates the empirical validity of these claims
in light of empirical evidence and theories coming from several
scientific and philosophical researches. It is important to emphasize
that the analysis conducted in this volume is mostly descriptive rather
than evaluative—it asks what the 'nature' of moral psychology is,
and especially whether, how, and to what extent it can change; many
normative and metaethical implications of these problems will not

be discussed here, nor will several issues related to the idea of moral progress.[1] From a descriptive point of view, morality and moral change are historical phenomena that can be studied empirically, suspending evaluative judgment about their goodness or desirability. This work adopts this descriptive approach.

Addressing the issue of the 'change potential' of moral psychology from a descriptive point of view is crucial because many ethical and political implications have recently arisen (and may arise) stemming from non-evaluative, empirical—allegedly scientific—assumptions about this matter. Indeed, recent empirical research in psychology and cognitive neuroscience, and more generally the growing scientific understanding of human cognition and behavior, continues to produce innovative empirically informed theoretical and normative proposals for psychological, moral, and social change (Greene 2013; Haidt 2012; Persson & Savulescu 2008; 2012; Crutchfield 2021; Levy 2021; Thaler & Sunstein 2008).

Consider, for instance, the recent debates on moral bio-enhancement and nudging, two of the most influential projects claiming to be based on empirical and experimental evidence from the cognitive and behavioral sciences aiming to improve people's behavior by steering it in morally preferable directions (Persson & Savulescu 2008; 2012; Crutchfield 2021; Levy 2021; Thaler & Sunstein 2008). Proposals like nudging and moral bio-enhancement aim to improve people's decisions and behavior claiming to be based on scientific evidence about the functioning of the human mind. Specifically, these projects emphasize that recent psychological and neuroscientific research highlight the systematic presence of countless biases and significant limitations in human cognition, decision-making, and behavior (Kahneman 2011; Sunstein 2005; Caviola et al. 2021). This evidence should, therefore, be taken into

---

1   Except for a few final passages in chapter 6. The concept of moral progress is evaluative and, in particular, implies positive evaluations of moral or social changes. Evaluative judgements and standards—and moral ones in particular—are notoriously often controversial; a defense or critique of specific normative or metaethical views of moral progress requires an ethical-philosophical analysis that is at least partly independent of the description of the dynamics of change. See Bina (2023; 2024a; 2024b).

account to build more realistic moral theories (Flanagan 1991; Songhorian 2019) and more effective strategies for individual and social change (Thaler & Sunstein 2008; Persson & Savulescu 2012; Levy 2021).

According to a bold version of this view, recent empirical evidence suggests that efforts aimed at correcting or mitigating the influence of distorting factors on human reasoning, behavior, and basic evaluative attitudes are ineffective and futile, as much of human psychology is deeply rooted in the brains and biology of *homo sapiens*—as well as of our closest non-human relatives—and is thus rigidly resistant to change (see, e.g., Schwitzgebel & Cushman 2015; Haidt 2001; 2012; Kahneman 2003; 2011; Klenk & Sauer 2021; Persson & Savulescu 2012; 2017; Sauer 2019; 2023). In particular, biases, heuristics, emotions, and other automatic, unconscious and often affectively charged cognitive processes belonging to the so-called 'system' or 'type' 1 of thinking and decision-making (Kahneman 2011), are seen as impenetrable, persistent, and resistant to change. In a sense, these processes are insensitive to reasons and evidence as visual illusions are: we cannot change our perceptual responses even if we know that objects are not the way we see them; we cannot see differently from how we see even if we try (Kahneman 2003). As far as moral cognition is concerned, a more moderate interpretation of this view suggests that active efforts aimed at bias reduction may be moderately effective, but still insufficient or too slow to address some of today's most pressing cooperative challenges, such as anthropogenic climate change or existential risks related to misuses of technology, such as AI (Persson & Savulescu 2012).

In light of these premises, several scholars have recently suggested that efforts to enhance people's epistemic and moral capacities with traditional means (like education) are ineffective and likely doomed to failure (Haidt 2001; 2012; Persson & Savulescu 2017; 2019; Klenk & Sauer 2021; Levy 2021). Instead of promoting or improving people's reasoning and decision-making abilities by reducing biases, prejudices, or self-interested motivations, several scholars have claimed that it would be better to 'bypass' conscious reasoning by intelligently leveraging biases, heuristics, selfish motivations, and other cognitive limitations to achieve the desired outcomes (Banaji & Greenwald 2013; Sauer 2019; Thaler & Sunstein 2008; Levy 2021).

Based on similar premises, a provocative yet influential proposal in the applied ethics debate—informed by research on the biological and neural bases of morality—argues for the need to develop biomedical moral enhancements (through drugs, genetic manipulations, neural implants) to tackle humanity most urgent moral challenges. Given that traditional means of moral education and reform are inadequate to bring about the large-scale psychological, epistemic, behavioral, and institutional changes needed to address critical issues such as climate change, mass migration, global poverty and inequality, and existential risks from technological advancements, we should prioritize the development of biomedical interventions to enhance individuals' behavior, emotions, and dispositions (Douglas 2008; Persson & Savulescu 2008; 2012; Jebari 2014), even if this means bypassing people's explicit moral deliberation, or restricting their freedom of choice (Persson & Savulescu 2012; Crutchfield 2021; Harris 2011; 2012; 2016; Reichlin 2019).

As we will see in the first part of the book, one of the main arguments supporting the view that human psychology and even moral beliefs (Street 2006; Joyce 2006; Guardo 2024) are so rigidly limited, tribalistic, biased and shortsighted is that these traits have been adaptive for most of human history: they were selected because they increased chances of survival and reproduction of those who possessed them, and this is why we still have them nowaydays (Barkow et al., 1992). This thesis should be considered alongside the widely supported claim that the evolution of biological traits is very slow. Mainstream evolutionary psychology defends this view, claiming that "our modern skulls house a Stone Age mind" (Cosmides & Tooby 1997, 85). Our moral psychology evolved as a response to universal existential challenges ("adaptive problems") in environments and societies that were very different from contemporary ones, with limited technologies, epistemic resources and chances of interaction:

In small, closely genetically related tribal groups, certain cooperative dispositions such as kin altruism or reciprocal altruism can be adaptive. Internally cooperative groups will enjoy a selective edge in intergroup competition for scarce resources in the environment of evolutionary adaptedness. Individuals who are disposed to care for their offspring and engage in reciprocal chains of sharing and helping increase the comparative frequency of their genes in the next generation. Unfortunately, this also means that our capacity to care for others is, and must be, limited. Natural selection operates on genes, and will tend to favor cooperative strategies that promote the proliferation of copies of alleles. This result cannot be achieved through cooperation that goes beyond relatives or reciprocators, because such forms of cooperation would result in costs that are not outweighed by any adaptive benefits, and are thus selected against. This means that evolutionary pressures have equipped our minds with a recalcitrant tendency to carve up the world in terms of an in- and an out-group. Benevolence exists, but *universal* benevolence is evolutionarily unstable. The very dispositions that make us cooperative also make us tribalistic (Sauer 2019, 155-156)

This view states that our limited cognitive infrastructure is the result of millennia of adaptation to ancestral environments. Yet, in a world that has changed dramatically and rapidly, our Stone Age minds struggle to address challenges that are vastly different from those they evolved to meet. (Savulescu & Persson 2012; Greene 2013; Singer 2005; 2011). Several influential scholars have claimed that we need to implement radical solutions to this problem, even if this means sacrificing valuable goods, like people's decisional autonomy (Persson & Savulescu 2012b; Thaler & Sunstein 2008).

For this reason, provocative and controversial reform projects such as moral enhancement and nudging have been widely debated and criticized. Critics, though, have predominantly questioned their normative assumptions and warned about their morally undesirable implications. For example, the presumption of the 'architects'[2] of these interventions to know better than their targets what is objectively

---

2   The idea of 'choice architecture' is a central concept in nudging, which posits that the way options are arranged or presented—e.g., their salience, proximity, ease of interaction, order of presentation—strongly influences agents' decisions. People tend to prefer and choose what is easier for them, even when this is defined by chance. Therefore, according to nudge

right or good for them has been criticized as a problematic violation of autonomy.[3] Another problem has been identified in the debatable inherent consequentialist approach of these projects, primarily aimed at the production of desired outcomes through interventions that 'bypass' agent's awareness and capacity to choose (Harris 2012; 2016; Rebonato 2012; Reichlin 2019; Songhorian et al. 2022). Curiously, much less attention has been dedicated to the scientific validity of the empirical premises on which these projects are based, and particularly to the idea that human psychology is hopelessly biased and rigidly limited *for evolutionary reasons*. This book aims to fill this gap.

The first chapter of the book is a very brief introduction to the study of morality from an evolutionary perspective. The literature on the subject has boomed over the past decades, and the history of the evolutionary study of cooperation and morality since Darwin is extremely rich and fascinating. In these introductory pages, readers will find references to both classic and more recent works to further explore several issues, but they should not expect to find a systematic review of the literature on the topic. Chapter 2 addresses the more specific view that constitutes the main critical target of the book, i.e., the idea that human moral psychology is rigidly bounded and biased due to the evolutionary history of our species. In chapter 3, I provide a brief overview of the most interesting theories and projects that claim to ground their views on moral, social and political change on evolutionary understandings of the moral mind. In chapter 4, I present evidence and arguments against the evolutionary premises these views rely on. Specifically, I argue

---

theorists, we should organize people's options—even spatially—so that the easiest to choose are also the best ones (Thaler & Sunstein 2008).

3   The idea that some individuals know what is best for people better than the subjects directly involved is technically known as *paternalism* (Dworkin 2002), based on the idea that a father (or parent) knows better than their children what is good for them, thereby justifying interference with their freedom of choice. Thaler & Sunstein, the first proponents of nudging, called their view *libertarian paternalism*: nudging involves a paternalistic push towards options that are deemed best, yet it preserves the possibility of choosing alternatives. The alternatives are not prohibited but merely made more difficult (Thaler & Sunstein 2008).

against the functionalist-adaptationist framework underpinning these evolutionary explanations, which asserts the existence of a universally shared and hardwired human capacity dedicated to moral cognition. Proponents of this view claim that this capacity was selected for its role in fostering cooperation in small groups, ultimately enhancing survival and reproductive success. I challenge this picture by showing that recent research from several disciplines indicates that the human cognitive and motivational infrastructure is not essentially and universally rigid and biased as many affirm, and that several institutional and epistemic conditions and socio-cultural dynamics can foster significant psychological and value change even in relatively short timeframes. In chapter 5, I consider the hypothesis that important aspects of human morality—particularly, certain forms of practical deliberation and moral reasoning—may be conceived as by-products of the biological and cultural selection of several psychological traits (both domain-general and domain-specific), which can favor their emergence and increased exercise independently of evolutionary pressures. Finally, in chapter 6 I address the question of whether moral reasoning—especially through the teaching of ethics—is as psychologically ineffective as many scholars have recently claimed, by discussing a few recent studies pointing to a more optimistic direction.

Acknowledgements

This book would not have been possible without the essential contributions of several remarkable persons. Many thanks to Michel Croce, Maria Silvia Vaccarezza, and Mario de Caro for making the publication of this book possible and for believing in me and in my work. Thanks to Josh Greene for many fundamental suggestions in the development of this work, and to Allen Buchanan and Hanno Sauer for helping me improve it. Thanks to Massimo Reichlin, Sarah Songhorian, and Francesca Guma for our collective work discussed in the final chapter of this book. A special thanks to my mother Monica for allowing me to work on parts of this book amidst the beautiful landscapes of Salina.

1.
EVOLUTION AND FUNCTION OF MORALITY

One of the most accredited ways to study morality from a descriptive and naturalistic perspective consists of looking at its evolutionary history to understand its biological function for the human species (and, perhaps, also for other species that share with us some basic elements of cognition and cooperation). From this perspective, morality should not be understood primarily on a conceptual level— e.g., by identifying formal or substantive properties that define it— but above all by shedding light on the role that it plays and the effects it produces within complex social systems. Over the past decades, the scientific study of the cooperative behavior of humans and other social animals has grown significantly, seeking to understand and explain the evolution of prosocial traits like altruism, empathy, trust, and the development of cooperative institutions; above all, through the lenses of the Darwinian theory of natural selection, enriched by contemporary developments in evolutionary and developmental biology.

One of the apparent paradox these disciplines have sought to explain is how traits and behaviors that benefit tothers (including entire groups) but are costly to the individuals exhibiting them— such as altruistic and cooperative behaviors—could have been selected by evolutionary mechanisms that generally favor traits that are directly advantageous to the individuals by enhancing their chances of survival and reproduction, thus passing on adaptive traits to future generations. In other words: how did morality, which entails individual costs, evolve, when evolution tends to favor what benefits the individuals?

One of the simplest and most widely accepted answers to this question is that moral behavior—caring for one's kins and kiths, respecting others, not lying, keeping promises—is ultimately advantageus because, despite the immediate costs it increases the reproductive fitness of individuals, hence passing those traits to the next generations. In other words, many evolutionary scientists and philosophers believe that morality is an *adaptation*, selected over millennia because (moderately) prosocial traits and institutions proved more beneficial for individuals and societies compared to those who exhibited different traits (e.g., more or less cooperative ones). This allowed moderately altruistic, empathetic, and cooperative individuals and groups to live longer, leave more offspring, and transmit these traits to future generations. In recent decades, many scholars have developed this adaptationist hypothesis about the evolution of morality in greater detail.

Morality appears to be a universal phenomenon observed across all contemporary and past cultures. It involves adherence to social rules independent of individual preferences, is supported and driven by other-directed and self-directed emotions and evaluations, and is reinforced by informal institutional sanctions. Anthropologist Oliver Scott Curry (2016) observed that there is a significant consensus among anthropologists, psychologists, and philosophers on the idea that morality is a direct product of natural selection, as it fosters cooperation and, consequently, enhances the reproductive fitness of individuals and groups. Several authors emphasize that this holds true for many aspects of morality, i.e., psychological traits, practices, norms, institutions, symbolic systems, beliefs, and principles (Curry 2016; Guardo 2024; Haidt 2012; Kitcher 2014; Tomasello & Vaish 2013). The adaptationist view of morality asserts that all these aspects can be explained evolutionarily: they have all proven advantageous for individuals and groups who exhibited them, which is why they have been selected and spread in human populations.

Some authors even suggested that the core principles upon which all moral systems are built may be somehow embedded in our genes (Joyce 2006; Street 2006; Hauser 2006; Mikhail 2007). Genetic information shape the way our brains and minds function, hence driving our moral judgments; this implies that a consistent part of morality may be innate. Children do not learn moral principles and behavior only (or mostly) through education and experience but more like they grow other parts of the body (like arms or hair); or similarly to how other animals come to behave in perfectly adaptive ways without anybody teaching them how to do (e.g., as baby turtles move towards the sea immediately after birth, or many animal species know how to avoid threats, build their nests, feed their babies, and so on). If this hypothesis is plausible, then, from a descriptive standpoint, morality can be fully naturalized. According to Curry, "The study of morality has finally become a branch of science" (Curry 2016, 29).

Let us now rapidly see some of the main adaptationist hypotheses about the evolution of morality.

Selfish genes and inclusive fitness. Some of the earliest and most influential formulations of the adaptationist view of morality can be found in the well-known theory of the *selfish gene* developed by the zoologist Richard Dawkins (1976) and in the provocative ideas of the entomologist Edward O. Wilson (1975), father of *sociobiology*, the closest antecedent to contemporary *evolutionary psychology*. Dawkins was among the first scholars to insist that the main level at which natural selection operates is not species, populations, or even individuals, but genes—the smallest units of transmission of biological information. For Dawkins, genes are "selfish" in the sense that their only purpose is to replicate and perpetuate themselves, even at the expense of the individuals who carry them, who are— according to Dawkins' evocative metaphor—merely vehicles that help selfish genes achieve their objective of spreading as much as possible. This view, Dawkins argues, can explain much of the altruistic behavior observed in nature. Altruism, by definition, is costly and may be harmful (and even fatal) to those exhibiting it.[1] However, the selection of altruistic traits and behaviors can be understood in light of the benefits that they bring to one's own's genes, rather than to the individuals themselves. It is no coincidence that the majority of significant altruistic behaviors in nature occur between

---

1   Even Darwin struggled to explain the sacrificial behaviors of certain social animals (such as some insect species), partly because he lacked a refined theory of heredity. Mendel's pioneering studies, which were roughly contemporary with Darwin's work, only began to circulate and be taken seriously decades later, in 1900.

parents and children, siblings, grandparents and grandchildren, and close relatives:[2] since they share much of one's genetic material, helping one's kin means benefiting one's own genes, increasing their chances of replicating and spreading. This idea has been called *inclusive fitness*: from a gene-centered perspective, behaviors that appear altruistic at the level of organisms are actually 'selfish', so that it is possible to favor one's own genes also by helping others.

It is important to note that when discussing biological selfishness and altruism we are not referring to conscious motives, but to evolutionarily ingrained tendencies—mostly instinctive and unconscious—that objectively benefit oneself or others, enhancing reproductive fitness. Therefore, most 'altruistic' behavior conceived in this sense does not stem from deliberate moral reasoning or concern for others. Rather, as E. O. Wilson observed, the psychological vehicles of altruism are "lying, pretense, and deceit, including self-deceit, because the actor is most convincing who believes that his performance is real" (Wilson 1978; passage reported in Ruse 2009, 336). In the famous words of the evolutionary biologist and philosopher Michael Ghiselin, "scratch an altruist and watch a hypocrite bleed" (Ghiselin 1974, 247).

The suggestion from several authors is that these biological pressures not only explain the presence of psychological traits, innate dispositions, institutions, and social norms that promote altruism toward close kin, but also extend to beliefs, principles, and even moral theories. In fact, altruism and care for close relatives are actually advocated as moral duties in virtually all human cultures (Curry 2016; Joyce 2006; Street 2006; Guardo 2024).[3]

---

2   According to Hamilton's rule, $rB > C$: for any altruistic behavior, the benefits provided to a relative (B) must outweigh the costs of performing that behavior (C), divided by the degree of genetic relatedness (r is 1/2 for parents, children, and siblings, 1/4 for grandparents and grandchildren, 1/8 for first cousins, and so on).

3   Curry reports several examples of this phenomenon: «"There is one duty so universal and obvious that it is seldom mentioned: the mother's duty to rear her children...Another duty...is incumbent on the married man: the protection and support of his family" (Westermarck, 1906); "the moral obligation for a mother to take care of her children...is a universal imperative' (Edel & Edel, 1959/1968). In Confucian ethics, 'Duty to the family trumped all other duties' (Fukuyama, 1996). Obligations to

Reciprocal altruism. While altruism, cooperation, and care among kin may constitute a significant part of moral behavior, the notions of kin selection and inclusive fitness do not seem sufficient to explain many other central aspects of human morality. Another kind of prosocial behavior that is highly relevant for any moral system and conception of morality has to do with forms of cooperation and mutual aid that many animals, including humans, display toward individuals with whom they are not related, and sometimes not even conspecific. These altruistic and trusting behaviors exist because they allow individuals to gain benefits that would otherwise be unattainable by their own, such as the practice of mutual parasite removal exhibited by many animal species (and even between species) (Trivers 1971). These behaviors are particularly significant in cognitively complex social animals, where individuals interact repeatedly to the point of remembering the benefits or wrongs (such as the failure to reciprocate) received from others, and anticipating the possibility of receiving (or not) further benefits. Many animals often need to coordinate with their conspecifics to achieve their goals (searching for food, fighting off enemy species and other environmental threats), and it is thus vital to learn who to trust based on past social interactions. This leads to the development of relationships such as friendships, alliances, coalitions, and power dynamics (Tooby & Cosmides 1996; Barclay 2016; Barclay & Willer 2007; Baumard et al. 2013).

Mathematical models of repeated social interactions (studied by evolutionary game theory) show that reciprocal altruism is an individually advantageous (and stable) strategy compared to unilaterally receiving the benefits of others' cooperative effort without bearing the costs of cooperating in return. In the long run, free riding—the pursuit of one's self-interest by exploiting the cooperative efforts of others without reciprocating—leads to negative consequences for everyone, while mutually agreeing to

---

family—an ethic of care, an obligation to distribute goods on the basis of need and relationship, not abstract rules—also figure prominently in some feminist moral philosophy (Noddings, 1978; Ruddick, 1980)"» (cited in Curry 2016, 31).

constrain one's behavior to help one another improves the situation for all (Trivers 1971; Axelrod 1984). In the language of evolutionary game theory, the best policy in repeated strategic interactions is the strategy known as *tit for tat*, according to which an agent cooperates on the first move and then mirrors the behavior of the other agents, cooperating if they cooperate and defecting if they defect.[4] It is important to note that reciprocity can also be indirect, meaning that the individual who cooperates does not need to be repaid by the same individuals who benefited from his effort: thanks to the reputational effects of gossip (Dunbar 2004; Nowak & Sigmund 2005), cooperative behavior ensures beneficial reciprocation from others, while those who do not cooperate get punished or excluded (see also Boyd & Richerson 1992).

As for kin altruism, adaptationist views suggest that these considerations explain not only the presence of innate and automatic dispositions towards direct and indirect reciprocity (Rand et al. 2012; 2014), but also beliefs, moral principles and theories that emphasize their importance and necessity; also these cultural products, adaptationists claim, were selected for their effect of reinforcing and justifying dispositions and behaviors that objectively increase reproductive fitness. As this theory predicts, reciprocity is a central principle in several ancient (Confucius 1994) and modern (Hobbes 1651/1958) moral philosophies, as well as in some of the most influential contemporary social theories (Rawls 1971; Gauthier 1987; Scanlon 1998); the golden rule is fundamental in the world's major religions (Chilton & Neusner 2009); in its negative form, reciprocity is a guiding principle of punishment and retribution theories from antiquity, as in the 'eye for an eye' rule in the Code of Hammurabi (Daly & Wilson, 1988).

Conflict resolution. Following Curry (2016), a third main effect of morality that seems to explain its natural selection appears connected to the ability to resolve conflicts, which can arise between living organisms due to competition for resources such as food, territory,

---

4   This is exceptionally well explained by the interactive game at https://ncase.me/trust/.

and sexual partners. Although these conflicts may appear to be 'zero-sum games', i.e., interactions where one side wins and the other loses, conflicts actually involve costs for all the competitors—in terms of time, energy, injuries, and suffering for oneself and others—that both sides have a shared interest in avoiding. For this reason, conflicts among animals are not modeled as zero-sum games but as 'hawk-dove' games, meaning nonzero-sum interactions in which, if both sides adopted a fully aggressive strategy, the interaction would result in the worst outcome for both (Maynard Smith & Price 1973). Often, conflicts offer opportunities for cooperation, shifting competition onto a less mutually destructive level. Simplifying, we will focus here on two main conflict resolution strategies of this kind: (a) displays of strength and submission, and (b) resource division.

(a) Instead of fighting, one option is for the competitors to display indicators of strength (combat ability, resource possession), and for the weaker side to submit to the stronger, for example, by conceding the contested stakes. The stronger party would still win, but in this way both would avoid the costs of an actual conflict (Gintis et al. 2001; Maynard Smith & Price 1973). These strategies are widespread in nature and, depending on the species, the display of power and aggressiveness (hawk-ish traits) can involve size, weight, or experience (Hardy & Briffa 2013; Riechert 1998); even altruistically, to benefit others such as relatives or partners, rather than oneself directly. Conversely, signals of submission (dove-ish traits) typically involve exaggerated concealment of those attributes or overt displays of their absence (Darwin 1872; Preuschoft & van Schaik 2000). Curry (2016) observes that humans have invented countless ways to display status and regulate social relations accordingly, such as caste systems, honors, etiquette rules, and dress codes. Males, in particular, often engage in conspicuous and costly displays of strength, skill, and resources, even altruistically, in the context of competition for mates (Hardy & Van Vugt 2006). Children spontaneously form dominance hierarchies relatively early in development (Edelman & Omark 1973).

Remember that the hypothesis under consideration suggests that certain biological adaptations, selected for their reproductive advantage, explain and directly influence not only human behaviors and practices but also beliefs, and even moral theories. In the case of hawk-ish and dove-ish traits, which are hypothetically selected as advantageous conflict-resolution strategies, the adaptationist view predicts that aggressive and submissive signals are constitutive parts of human morality. In fact, displays of strength, courage, heroism, generosity, and magnanimity, on the one hand, and submission traits like humility, deference, respect, and obedience, on the other, are considered character virtues in nearly all cultures worldwide (Curry 2016).

(b) If the contested resource is divisible (such as territory or the spoils of a hunt), game theory models the situation as a bargaining problem (Nash 1950). In these cases, a natural strategy is to divide the resource in proportion to the bargaining power of the parties involved (Skyrms 1996). In the case of equally powerful individuals, this leads to egalitarian divisions (Maynard Smith 1982). Ethnographic studies show that hunter-gatherer societies, where the first moral norms were likely originally selected (Tomasello 2016), were strongly egalitarian. Any violation of egalitarian principles, such as attempts to exercise excessive authority and dominance over others, were punished with social exclusion and even execution (Boehm 2012; 2001). Despite significant cultural and individual differences, the practice and belief in the justice of distributing resources according to merit and needs are widespread across all human societies. In economic games, dividing resources equally is a spontaneous decision-making rule that is widely observed across cultures (Güth et al. 1982; Henrich et al. 2005); egalitarian principles are present in all religious and philosophical moral systems throughout human history, as the theory predicts.

In conclusion, the adaptationist hypothesis, which posits that morality was selected for its fitness-enhancing effects through the promotion of cooperation, predicts that people's feelings, behaviors, and beliefs about the goodness and rightness of specific character traits and actions can be explained by the fitness benefits associated with those dispositions, behaviors, and beliefs. Indeed, helping family members, being loyal, honest, and fair with people and groups, reciprocating favors, being courageous, respecting authority, acknowledging merit, and fairly dividing contested resources are almost universally considered morally good or just. Failure to observe these forms of cooperation—e.g., by neglecting family, betraying one's group, cheating, being coward, disrespecting authority, being unfair or overbearing, and stealing—is almost universally regarded as morally bad (Curry 2016).

According to the view sketched out so far, morality and its many components—moral emotions, normative cognition (i.e., following social rules and punishing violators), systems of virtues, moral principles and theories, etc.—have all been selected because of the fitness-enhancing effects that these prosocial traits produced for millennia of evolution. In particular, many scholars believe that enhancing cooperation is the *function* of morality:

> Essentially, moral judgments are the product of a mechanism that enables groups of interacting individuals to coordinate their actions and emotions to mutual advantage. The function of moral habits is thus to generate patterns of cooperative action and emotion that are mutually beneficial (Sinclair 2012, 14);

> The function of morality is to increase social cohesion through the amplification of our psychological dispositions towards altruism (Kitcher 2005, 178).

According to this view, moral traits and institutions can be explained by the advantage they provided in response to social and environmental challenges of existential importance over hundreds of thousands, perhaps millions of years (Barkow et al. 1992; Tomasello 2018). But is a response to those ancestral existential problems still the main function of morality in contemporary societies? Does morality continue to serve its 'original' function today or could its function have changed, especially in light of new environmental and social conditions and challenges? According to Philip Kitcher, one of the most authoritative scholars on this topic and a defender of a functionalist-adaptationist theory of morality,

> The current situation of humanity is analogous to the one that originally sparked the ethical project. As it was in the beginning, so it is now: the conflicts that affected the lives of our ancestors are reflected in the contemporary hostilities within the human population. From this

perspective, the original function of ethics, which was to remedy the deficiencies of altruism, remains primary (Kitcher 2011, 8).

Kitcher claims that the current function of morality is largely the same that it was tens of thousands of years ago: to compensate for the limitations of human psychology and altruism, to curb selfish and aggressive instincts, and to promote cooperation within small groups of individuals. But what does it mean to say that morality has a function—in this case, the function of increasing cooperation and therefore fitness? What do we mean when we talk about the function of a biological trait or product of culture?

According to a classic, very minimal and general definition, the function of an entity x can be understood as the effect that x has in a system, which explains why x persists within it (Wright 1976). More specifically, according to *etiological* theories of function, x has a certain function due to the effects that x produced over its history: "the central element of the etiological approach should be seen as the simple idea that a function of a trait is the effect for which that trait was selected" (Neander 1991, 459). Several scholars have proposed etiological explanations of this kind for the emergence and persistence of biological and cultural traits and phenomena, as well as for institutions and artifacts (Millikan 1984; Neander 1991; Kitcher 1993). For example, a biological trait common to many species, such as nostrils, has the function of perceiving odors because perceiving odors is an effect of the nostrils that has causally contributed to their transmission through generations of organisms. Another example may be that of an institution like money, which has the function of mediating exchanges because mediating exchanges is a function of money that has enabled its transmission over generations. Similarly, the adaptationist approach to morality suggests that moral cognition and institutions have the function of enhancing cooperation because enhancing cooperation is an effect of moral cognition and institutions that has causally contributed to their transmission over generations. Modest prosocial traits, such as dispositions to empathize and cooperate with limited groups of people conferred an advantage to individuals and groups who possessed them, and this contributed to their transmission and persistence over generations. At the same time, however, ethnographic, anthropological and psychological research reports that human cognition is not as good at sustaining cooperation *between* groups (Böhm et al. 2020; Greene 2013; Tomasello 2016).

By combining available evidence with an etiological theory of function, evolutionary psychologists hypothesize that several biases, social heuristics, and psychological traits such as in-group favoritism, conformism, scope neglect, limited moral concern (etc.) that humans still widely display nowadays have been selected throughout evolution because they contributed to enhancing the reproductive fitness of our ancestors (Haselton & Nettle 2006). In the environment of evolutionary adaptedness (EEA), limited prosocial traits likely had the advantage of protecting early humans from several existential threats, e.g., to physical integrity—from infectious diseases or personal violence—and material resources (Choi & Bowles 2007; Faulkner et al. 2004; Kurzban & Leary 2001; Navarrete & Fessler 2006; McDonald et al. 2012; Neuberg & Schaller 2016; Oaten et al. 2011; Persson & Savulescu 2012, 38; Tomasello 2016).

According to evolutionary psychology (EP), and to evolutionary accounts of morality that rely on its core claims, the reason why greater prosocial, inclusivist, and cooperative dispositions, and more sophisticated, unbiased, and farsighted deliberative skills and institutions have *not* been selected for is that their existential costs would have significantly exceeded their benefits in the EEA. Human beings possessing too inclusive, reflective or longtermist attitudes were likely eliminated in the Pleistocene, while more parochial, intolerant, (selectively) hostile, decisive and impulsive individuals survived; cognitive and behavioral traits that allowed humans to deal more efficiently with life-or-death environmental and social challenges were transmitted over generations and selected, while costly and inefficient ones were not, because their bearers had lower chances of survival and reproduction (Haselton & Nettle 2006; Tomasello 2018; Sauer 2019).

In other words, according to EP, moral cognition and morality essentially evolved as intra-group, short-sighted, and short-termist social devices. This view, of course, is neither recent nor isolated. Authoritative scholars from several scientific fields have defended similar positions in the past decades. For instance, in *The Limits of Altruism*, ecologist Garrett Hardin stated that morality cannot but exist "on a small scale, over the short term, in certain circumstances and within small, intimate groups" (1977, 26). In *The Selfish Gene*, zoologist Richard Dawkins claimed that "Much as we might wish to believe otherwise, universal love and the welfare of the species as a whole are concepts which simply do not make evolutionary sense" (1976, 2-3). Combine these views with the idea that functional explanations in biology are typically associated with traits' rigidity and resistance to change (cf. Buchanan & Powell 2015, 47), and we have a case for a hard-wired parochial, exclusivist and shortsighted social and moral psychology. On these grounds, evolutionary psychologists have explicitly expressed skepticism about the possibility of significant mental plasticity (Barkow et al. 1992, 39; Pinker 2002). On the same basis, several thinkers have also recently questioned the possibility of robust psychological moral change (Asma 2012; Haidt 2012; Sauer 2019; 2023; Persson & Savulescu 2017; Levy 2021; for a review, see Buchanan & Powell 2015).[5]

Note that the fact that some traits were selected because of the advantages they conferred to generations of our ancestors in the EEA by no means implies that these traits are still adaptive nowadays (evolutionary psychologists tend to agree on this point). On the contrary, traits that evolved in radically different circumstances

---

5   One of the main claims of classic evolutionary psychology is that the mind is modular: "an array of psychological mechanisms (modules) that is universal among Homo sapiens" (Symons 1992, 139), selected for their adaptedness in the EEA. According to this view the mind is like a Swiss Army knife: a combination of different tools performing specific functions. For evolutionary psychologists, modules of the mind are many, innate, and domain-specific. They are also 'informationally encapsulated', i.e., impenetrable by the cognitive processes generally involved in the activation of other modules. The modularity of mind hypothesis was first formulated by Fodor (1983), though he conceived only 'low-level' peripheral cognitive systems as modular (e.g., vision and perception). Fodor's hypothesis has been later extended to other cognitive systems— the *massive modularity* hypothesis—by Cosmides & Tooby (1992; 1997), Pinker (1997), Samuels (1998). For critiques of this hypothesis, see Prinz (2006b), Sterelny (2010), Pietraszewski & Wertz (2022).

can be even very counterproductive and dangerous in modern environments and societies. This problem is technically known as *evolutionary mismatch*: "Our minds are adapted to the small foraging bands in which our family spent ninety-nine percent of its existence, not to the topsy-turvy contingencies we have created since the agricultural and industrial revolutions" (Pinker 1997, 207; see also Li et al. 2017).[6]

Given these considerations, skeptical views about the feasibility and effectiveness of traditional strategies for moral reform have been recently offered to the philosophical debate. To illustrate some of the possible practical implications of this skeptical temperament, in the next section I discuss two recent accounts which emblematically rely on the hard-wiring thesis. As stated above, I will not challenge either the ethical-philosophical content nor the moral implications of these accounts. My aim here is rather to show that the theoretical and practical conclusions they draw are untenable, since one of their main empirical premises—the hard-wiring thesis—is empirically unsupported.[7]

Before proceeding, a final consideration about the meaning and scope of evolutionary explanations of morality is in order. Recall that advocates of the hard-wiring thesis claim that biases and tribalistic attitudes are so hard-wired in our cognitive architecture that it is virtually impossible to overcome or mitigate their influence, at least

---

6   However, some scholars emphasize that several cognitive traits and mechanisms that many see as the problematic legacy of human adaptation to radically different environments are still very adaptive nowadays (Gigerenzer 2007; Gigerenzer et al. 2011; Page 2022; Railton 2014; 2017).

7   Another, more moderate way to frame this problem may be to state not that human moral psychology is either hard-wired or it is not, but rather that the influence of our evolved traits and biases (and of our evolutionary history more in general) on human cognition and behavior is more or less significant (so disagreement would be about grade rather than being an 'all or nothing' issue). Of course, however, it would be hard to quantify such an influence (10, 50, 80%?). Hence, for argument's sake, I will stick to the hard-wiring formula; but the unconvinced reader could substitute 'hard-wiring' with 'steep-climbing'. Thanks to Josh Greene for making me clarify this point.

with ordinary socio-cultural tools such as education or reasoning. These evolved shortcomings, they argue, constrain not only (i) human psychology and motivation, but also (ii) moralities—conceived as historically realized systems of practices—and (iii) the content of moral beliefs as well as that of more systematic philosophical ethical theories (see, e.g., Haidt 2012; Greene 2007; Schwitzgebel & Cushman 2015; Persson & Savulescu 2012; 2017; Street 2006). According to evolutionary psychology, in fact, even culture and reasoning are the direct "product of evolved psychological mechanisms" (Tooby & Cosmides 1992, 24; see also Haidt 2012; Mercier & Sperber 2017; Sperber 1996; Street 2006).

Some advocates of moral hard-wiring acknowledge that human morality may not be fully explained by adaptationist evolutionary accounts. Persson and Savulescu, for instance, concede that morality "is also formed by socio-cultural factors and reasoning [...] But while evolutionary considerations cannot explain these cognitive or doxastic elements of morality [...] they can explain a number of motivational or non-cognitive elements of our moral psychology, and why they can have a hard time catching up with the former elements" (2017, 290). However, as recent experimental research points out, cognitive and doxastic elements of morality often depend on motivational or 'non-cognitive' processes (Bago & De Neys 2019; Bialek & De Neys 2017; Campbell & Kumar 2012; Cushman 2013; Damasio 1994; Greene et al. 2001; Greene 2007; Haidt 2001; 2012; Prinz 2006a; 2007).[8]

Hence, if we accept Persson and Savulescu's claim that evolutionary explanations mostly account for motivational and 'non-cognitive' aspects of our moral psychology (i), then we should also accept that 'cognitive' or doxastic aspects of morality (ii-iii) might, at least partially, be explained by evolutionary considerations. Unsurprisingly, in several works the authors state that evolved natural inclinations—such as the universal human preference for indirect harm—significantly affect the very content of our ethical theories (Persson & Savulescu 2012). If this were the case, then the

---

8   On the use of 'cognitive' and 'non-cognitive' in moral psychology, see
     Greene (2007, 40-41).

fact that moral cognition still depends on adaptations to existential challenges in the EEA would rigidly constrain not only motivational aspects of morality, but also the content of moral beliefs, principles, and theories (see, e.g., Curry 2016; Greene 2007; Street 2006). If this view were correct, the possibility of significant moral change (at all the aforementioned levels) would be considerably reduced.

Having clarified this, the reader should now have the basic foundational elements to understand the main theses that constitute the primary focus of this book.

2.
STONE AGE MINDS AND
MORAL HARD-WIRING

In contemporary discussions in empirically informed philosophy, as well as in the cognitive and social sciences, several scholars have claimed that the psychological changes necessary to address the most pressing collective problems of our time, and to comply with demanding normative standards and requirements, are virtually impossible for human beings to achieve—at least through ordinary socio-cultural means and projects aimed at fostering epistemic, moral, and social improvement (see Sauer 2019; Persson & Savulescu 2017; 2019; Thaler & Sunstein 2008; Levy 2021). At the core of this pessimistic view lies the idea that the cognitive infrastructure of human beings is rigidly shaped and constrained by the evolutionary history of our species (Barkow et al. 1992; Haidt 2012; Haselton & Nettle 2006; Street 2006; Clark & Winegard 2020; Clark et al. 2019; see also Buchanan & Powell 2015; 2018; and Buchanan 2020 for further critical discussions). As anticipated, according to this view, the human brain and mind have evolved up to their current configuration because they allowed humans to adaptively respond to existential threats and cooperative problems in pre-modern environments and societies, mostly over the late Pleistocene. This is why, according to many scholars, humans are nowadays ill-prepared to face complex problems that recent developments and conditions of life created: our minds were not selected to face challenges of this scale.

More specifically, several authors have argued that the psychological and epistemic changes that would be necessary to effectively address some of the most pressing cooperative problems of our time—intergroup conflicts between populations and cultures, global poverty and inequalities, climate change, regulation and management of AI, and other significant existential risks—are virtually impossible for our species, because human cognition is essentially tribalistic, exclusive, and short-sighted (Clark et al. 2019; Haidt 2012; Persson & Savulescu 2017). Traditional means for moral and intellectual improvement and social reform are clearly ineffective in tackling these issues, not only because they require too long to produce the desired effects, but also because they offer no guarantee of success (Klenk & Sauer 2021; Persson & Savulescu 2012).

Buchanan and Powell (2015; 2018) distinguished the advocates of this view into evolutionary 'conservatives' and evolutionary 'liberals', based on different normative implications that scholars have derived from accepting the same empirical premise.

Evolutionary conservatives. Evo-conservatives believe that human nature is fixed and essentially unchangeable, and appeal to evolutionary explanations to defend pessimistic or conservative views on moral and social change (Arnhart 2005; Asma 2012; Fukuyama 2002; Goldsmith & Posner 2005; Haidt 2012). Specifically, they argue that human psychology cannot be extended beyond certain limits that have already been largely reached (cf. Sauer 2019). Therefore, both normative moral and political theories and socio-political ideals and projects should be adapted to this fact to be achievable (or realistic). In particular, as Buchanan and Powell observe,

> Evoconservatives can be seen as attempting to heed the principle of minimal psychological realism (PMPR) [...]. The PMPR holds that moral theory and moralities should take the psychological capacities of human beings into account in framing their conceptions of moral principles, duties, and virtues. "Taking into account" our psychological capacities here is usually understood to mean recognizing the empirically evidenced limitations of those capacities. [...] our moral and political theories must be "motivationally reasonable", both with respect to their prescriptions for individual behavior and the institutions they require we adopt. A moral ideal satisfies the PMPR if its prescriptions are presently realizable by "all biologically normal human beings" or "asymptotically

realizable" by their descendants. The PMPR can thus be seen as the naturalizing philosopher's version of the slogan "ought implies can." Evoconservatives appear to be taking the PMPR seriously. They think that moralities and institutions should be realistic in the sense that they should not overestimate human abilities to extend sympathy—and more fundamentally, moral community—to out-groups. They reason that because our moral traits are products of selection in the EEA, or constrained by-products of the same, our capacities for other-regard are highly circumscribed (Buchanan & Powell 2015, 65-66).

In light of this assumption, evolutionary conservatives claim that

The ecological challenges faced by our distant ancestors generated selective pressures for evaluative tendencies that limit moral obligations to members of one's kin, group, tribe, or nation—and these presumed facts about human evolutionary history significantly constrain the shape of plausible morals and the range of concern that can be shown for others. This, in turn, suggests that cosmopolitan and inclusivist moral principles are neither appropriate nor realistic for beings like us [...]

Evo-conservatives believe that there are significant evolved psychological constraints on the shape of human morality, that these constraints are essentially fixed, and that they result in a scope of other-regard that is effectively restricted to in-groups. The chief "improvement" of evo-conservatism over traditional conservative philosophies is that it appeals to contemporary evolutionary psychology to ground its empirical claims about the moral limitations of human nature. Evoconservatives, then, hold that the content of morality—in particular, the scope of moral duties and the class of beings who are recognized as having moral standing—is severely constrained due to evolutionary history. This in turn limits the set of social practices and institutions that are feasible (Buchanan & Powell 2015, 44, 45).[1]

---

1   Some influential scholars holding such a conservative view have claimed that "We should not expect individual altruism to extend to people who are physically and culturally more distant" (Goldmith & Posner 2005, 212); or that "It would be nice to believe that we humans were designed to love everyone unconditionally. Nice, but rather unlikely from an evolutionary perspective. Parochial love—love within groups—amplified by similarity, a sense of shared fate, and the suppression of free riders, may be the most we can accomplish" (Haidt 2012, 245).

As Buchanan and Powell highlight, evo-conservatives not only believe that it is implausible to consider and treat all human beings as moral equals, but also justify treating many subjects (both humans and non-humans) as lacking any dignity or moral consideration at all (2015, 46). This conservative view, based on the impossibility of extending cooperation and moral consideration beyond one's own limited natural inclinations, capacities, relationships and bonds, often implies attributing great importance to direct reciprocity in the moral sphere, justifying it mostly on the basis of self-interest:

> the only sort of morality that humans are capable of engaging in, in any sustained and robust way, is what we will refer to as morality as cooperative group reciprocity. According to morality as cooperative group reciprocity theories, moral standing is something that members of a cooperative group confer on one another—and only on one another. Individuals excluded from this reciprocal arrangement have no moral standing at all, and hence there are no moral duties constraining how out-group members should be treated. Moral status is conferred on individuals who can either disrupt or contribute to cooperation—that is, on the basis of "strategic capacities" relative to a cooperative scheme [...]. The strategic conception of morality gels with, and is arguably central to, evolutionary theories of morality. It is not surprising, therefore, that evolutionary theorists have explicitly linked the selectionist account to a strategic, prudence-based theory of morality, such as that of Gauthier. Furthermore, the strategic conception has a radical implication: it denies moral status to individuals within the group if they lack the ability to harm or to benefit others in the group, as is the case with severely disabled individuals (ibid., 48).[2]

Evolutionary liberals. Based on the same empirical premise, other scholars have drawn diametrically opposed normative conclusions. Evo-liberals, too, argue that available efforts aimed at modifying, correcting, and improving people's minds and behavior—such as promoting greater inclusivity, prosociality, better motivation, and moral reasoning skills—through traditional means like education and other forms of incentives have proven, and seem destined to remain, ineffective. However, this does not mean that moral change

---

2   The reference is here to Gauthier (1987).

is impossible. Alternative strategies for moral reform may, in fact, prove far more effective than those attempted so far and should be seriously considered, especially given the urgency of the existential problems humanity faces, and in light of new scientific evidence and opportunities enabled by recent technological advancements.

Like evo-conservatives, evo-liberals believe that human psychology is significantly influenced and constrained by our evolutionary history, and argue that the ordinary cultural tools at our disposal (which have already been extensively tested) either do not work or their effect is negligible for tackling challenges like reducing intergroup conflict, mitigating global warming, facilitating integration, social justice, gender equality, animal well-being, and so forth.

However, unlike evo-conservatives, evo-liberals argue that human psychology and moral behavior can—and must—be modified, even quite radically, though not through traditional means. To address the major moral and socio-political challenges of our time, influential scholars have extensively argued that we must invest in and implementing alternative, evidence-based strategies that can more effectively foster psychological moral change. The prominent example case of this view is the recent defense of the necessity for moral bioenhancement (Crutchfield 2021; Douglas 2008; Persson & Savulescu 2008; 2012; 2017). One of the fundamental ideas behind this proposal is that human psychology is ill-prepared to address present and future challenges that humanity is facing. Today's world is radically different from the pre-modern socio-ecological conditions in which our cognitive infrastructure was selected and assumed its current configuration. New scenarios and opportunities raise unprecedented moral challenges and pose novel normative demands, but "humans by nature are not equipped with a moral psychology capable of coping with the moral problems these new conditions of life create" (Persson & Savulescu 2012, 1). The following passage from Persson and Savulescu is worth quoting at length to better convey their view in their own words:

> For most of the time the human species has existed, human beings have lived in comparatively small and close-knit societies, with primitive

technology that enabled them to affect only their most immediate environment. Their moral psychology adapted to make them fit to live in these conditions. This moral psychology is "myopic," restricted to concern about people in the neighborhood and the immediate future. But through science and technology, humans have radically changed their living conditions, while their moral psychology has remained fundamentally the same throughout this technological and social evolution, which continues at an accelerating speed. Human beings now live in societies with millions of citizens and with an advanced scientific technology which enables them to exercise an influence that extends all over the world and far into the future. This is leading to increasing environmental degradation and to harmful climate change. The advanced scientific technology has also equipped human beings with nuclear and biological weapons of mass destruction which might be used by states in wars over dwindling natural resources or by terrorists. Liberal democracies cannot overcome these problems by developing novel technology. What is needed is an enhancement of the moral dispositions of their citizens, an extension of their moral concern beyond a small circle of personal acquaintances, including those existing further in the future. The expansion of our powers of action as the result of technological progress must be balanced by a moral enhancement on our part. Otherwise, our civilization, we argued, is itself at risk. It is doubtful whether this moral enhancement could be accomplished by means of traditional moral education. There is therefore ample reason to explore the prospects of moral enhancement by biomedical means (Persson & Savulescu 2012, 399-400).

A less radical but still moderately optimistic view about the possibility of moral change despite our evolved psychological constraints has been proposed by Hanno Sauer (2019). Sauer, too, thinks that human moral psychology cannot be stretched beyond certain limits, which have already been largely reached. For this reason, he suggests that to foster the socio-moral changes we need or desire we should bypass, rather than stretch, the evolved limits of our psychology. He proposes leveraging human cognitive and motivational shortcomings—such as self-interest, competitiveness, tribalism, and the desire for power—by designing epistemic, social, and institutional environments that facilitate and promote behaviors and outcomes that are deemed better (Sauer 2019; Thaler & Sunstein 2008; Levy 2021). According to Sauer, even though human cognitive abilities are significantly constrained by evolution, "we should not expect our individual moral psychology to play a major role in promoting or sustaining moral progress" (158); we should "work around, rather than further stretch, the constraints of our evolutionary psychology to make moral progress possible" (153), using "smart institutional solutions" (163). Similarly, according to Neil Levy, we should not so much focus on the cultivation of individual (intellectual or moral) virtues, but instead build a system of nudges—non-monetary incentives and stimuli—to better understand ourselves and the world around us, navigating and cleaning up polluted epistemic environments (Levy 2021).

Sauer calls this approach "institutional bypassing" (2019, 162). His proposal is based on the idea that significant moral changes occur without involving significant shifts in people's minds or psychology, such as their abilities for information processing, conceptual understanding (cf. Moody-Adams 1999; Severini 2021; Bina et al. 2024), moral consistency reasoning (Campbell & Kumar 2012), moral justification (Songhorian et al. 2022), sympathetic imagination, bias reduction (Schaefer & Savulescu 2019), emotional regulation (De Caro et al., forthcoming), to mention just a few. According to advocates of institutional bypassing like Sauer and Levy, the extraordinary moral change that societies have been experiencing throughout (especially recent) history primarily depends on, and consists of, the development of supra-individual institutions capable of ensuring better social cooperation, rather than requiring changes in individual minds:

> Modern humans are hypersocial in a way that cannot be attributed to changes in our psychological capacities because these developments are too recent. Cooperation in large-scale societies, if it had to reach through individual minds to work, would impose unbearably heavy motivational burdens on individual people. It is almost impossible to motivate people to cooperate with strangers on the other side of the planet out of the goodness of their hearts. There are evolutionary limits to human inclusiveness. Does this mean that evolutionary conservatives are right, and large-scale cooperation is not a feasible political ideal? Of course not. There is an institutional arrangement—the market—that provides a workaround. It facilitates extensive chains of cooperation,

and incentives to benefit others, without relying on the baker's (or anyone's!) benevolence (Sauer 2019, 163; see also Sauer 2023, Introduction and chapter 4).

To strengthen his point, Sauer adds that

the chains of cooperation and mutual benefit between millions of people achieved by market institutions have not been brought about by such transformations, and do not depend on them. Rather, the most successful (both in terms of outcome and further scalability) modern institutions achieve certain moral gains—securing cooperation and reciprocal benefit between distant strangers—without the involvement of *any motivation whatsoever* to cooperate with or benefit others [...] the heavy lifting in this "expansion" of the circle of cooperation is done by an institutional arrangement that does indeed bypass, rather than modify, our dispositions. And the level of cooperativeness so achieved is clearly beyond the limits of what even the most optimistic assessment of our onboard psychological resources could consider feasible. The point generalizes. The market is merely one example for how clever institutional design can render evolved psychological constraints irrelevant. Democratic institutions, for instance, also redirect otherwise morally dubious motives towards socially beneficial goals. The hunger for power, prestige, and dominance may have an evolutionary rationale. Under normal conditions, these dispositions typically lead to socially harmful attempts to benefit oneself, one's family, and one's loyal allies. But when the control of the monopoly in (legitimate) violence is tied to the ability to win elections, one's Machiavellian goals have to become at least somewhat aligned with the interests of the majority. [...] frequently, the best way of dealing with undesirable psychological dispositions (such as selfishness or the will to power) is not to bludgeon them into shape, but to harness their force (Sauer 2019, 164-165).

It should now be clear how many different implications have been (and can be) drawn from the same empirical premise about the evolutionary limits that characterize moral psychology and its resistance to change. Evo-conservatives contend that there is nothing we can do to modify our evolved nature, claiming that significantly more inclusive, cooperative, and prosocial changes are out of reach for limited beings like us. On the other hand, evo-liberals, and especially advocates of moral enhancement, believe that such limits must be forced and altered through invasive interventions. Others, like Sauer, argue that our evolved limits are irrelevant, and may be even advantageous, asserting that the most significant moral changes in history have been primarily *institutional* rather than *psychological*; there is no need to force human psychology (e.g., to extend our empathic, cooperative, and altruistic dispositions), because there is no reason to believe that psychology and motivation play any significant role in moral change.

Now, as already stated, I am not interested in discussing here the ethical assumptions and implications of these accounts of moral change. I am primarily interested in whether the empirical thesis on which these accounts are based—the hard-wiring thesis—is correct. In the following sections, I will show that the idea that human beings are doomed to be tribalistic, biased and shortsighted contrast with empirical evidence and theoretical developments in several scientific and philosophical fields. A potential response to my objections could be that they are based on a misunderstanding of the notions of evolutionary influences on behavior and evolved innate predispositions. According to this reply, evo-conservatives and evo-liberals would not be claiming that human psychology is permanently fixed and completely insensitive to change. Evo-liberals, in particular, do not deny that psychological change is, in principle, possible; more modestly, what they insist on is that significant psychological change would take too long and too much effort to be sufficiently effective, widespread, and stable to tackle some of the major and most urgent moral problem of our time. The evidence I will examine in the following sections is organized from the longest to the shortest period of time required for psychological moral change to occur. This evidence show that several socio-cultural factors can significantly shape human moral cognition and behavior, both over centuries and within a single lifetime.

3.
AGAINST MORAL HARD-WIRING

3.1. *Are morality and moral cognition adaptations?*

A first objection to the hard-wiring thesis stems from a general skepticism towards the explanatory power of methods and hypotheses of evolutionary psychology (EP). Specifically, some perplexities are addressed to the reliability of EP's theoretical tools in understanding social and moral cognition in ecological, material, structural, and epistemic conditions which radically differ from the Environment of Evolutionary Adaptedness (EEA), i.e., the late Pleistocene. A comprehensive critique of EP lies, however, beyond the scope of this work.[1] I will thus limit my considerations to the idea that human moral and prosocial cognition and behavior could be understood and explained through the core methodologies, assumptions, and theoretical claims of classic EP.

How can we assess whether and how some definitory traits of a *specifically moral* kind of cognition technically evolved? As stated above, EP approaches the study and explanation of cognitive and behavioral traits as evolutionary biology seeks to explain the evolution of any other biological trait. Biological traits can evolve in

---

[1] One of the most extensive critiques of evolutionary psychology has been formulated by Buller (2005). See also Gould & Lewontin (1979) for a classical critique of the abuses of adaptationist/selectionist explanations of biological, psychological and behavioral traits. According to Gould and Lewontin, evolutionary psychologists often make up unproven 'just-so-stories' tracing back current traits to functional responses to environmental challenges that our ancestors would have faced in the Pleistocene.

several ways: for the current purposes, let us focus on two of them, *adaptations* and *exaptations*.

As discussed in the previous section, evolutionary psychologists tend to conceive of morality and moral cognition as evolutionary adaptations, i.e., as traits directly selected by evolutionary pressures due to their role in enhancing cooperation and reciprocal benefits in realtively small and closely genetically realted groups, thereby increasing chances of survival and reproductive success. Biological traits are *adaptations* when they get selected because they turn out to be fitness-enhancing, i.e., individuals displaying a trait leave more descendants (compared to those who lack it) to whom the trait is transmitted.

On the other hand, *exaptations* are evolutionary by-products. Some traits selected for their fitness-enhancing contribution— e.g., because they facilitate addressing more efficiently specific ecological challenges—can later prove useful for responding to even radically different problems, for addressing which they are subsequently coopted. In one of the most famous papers in the history of evolutionary theory, Gould and Lewontin (1979) referred to this phenomenon as "secondary adaptation" (596), or "the fruitful use of available parts" (584). The term *exaptations* was later coined by Gould and Vrba (1982) to refer to traits "evolved for other usages (or for no function at all), and later 'coopted' for their current role" (6).[2]

Hence, only adaptations can be understood, strictly speaking, as *direct* results of natural selection. But how can we know whether a trait is an evolutionary adaptation, i.e., if it was selected because of its fitness-enhancing contribution? Evolutionists agree that some relatively uncontroversial indicators can help find out whether or not

---

2   For instance, feathers likely evolved in the first place to keep the body warm, and only later were co-opted for flying. Some plants likely used to secrete resins in the first place to defend against herbivores, and only later resins became a reward for pollinators (Garson 2008). Several cultural human activities (e.g., literature) can also be considered exaptations, since they can be conceived as by-products of the evolution of other forms of intelligence (see Ayala 2010; Buss et al. 1998; Gould & Lewontin 1979).

a trait can be considered an adaptation. Let's briefly examine a few of the most important ones. First, there are good reasons to hold a trait an adaptation if we can clearly identify a *specific function* that explains its selection, transmission and persistence over generations of organisms. For instance, as far as cognitive and behavioral traits are concerned, classic evolutionary psychology tends to see the mind as composed of domain-specific modules, each of which can be given a clear functional explanation, which can be traced back to adaptive responses to vital ecological challenges in the EEA (Barkow et al. 1992).

Other important indicators for inferring the evolutionary adaptedness of a trait are its antiquity, universality, and early ontogenetic development. These features often co-occur. For instance, traits that are universally shared by members of a species — including psychological ones, such as the ability to learn any possible language (Chomsky 1975)—generally also develop very early in life. This phenomenon can be explained by hypothesizing either that (a) these traits are easily acquired as by-products of the ontogenetic development of other traits (e.g., they are learned after having developed other, domain-general cognitive abilities), or (b) that they are innate,[3] i.e., the result of selective pressures operating on specific ontogenetic developmental pathways. According to EP, evolved modules of the human mind satisfy all these conditions: they are evolutionarily old, universal across societies and cultures, and develop very early in life, independently of the acquisition of other psychological capacities (Barkow et al. 1992; Tooby & Cosmides 1990). Hence, they can likely be considered adaptations.

Now, to evaluate if the hard-wiring thesis is correct—i.e., whether the function of moral cognition and morality remains solving small-group cooperative problems, the function for which they have been selected—we may assess whether they meet the aforementioned conditions for being considered evolutionary adaptations. Is

---

3   The link between adaptations and innateness is partly problematic since, e.g., innate traits like genetic diseases are not adaptations, while the development of certain adaptive traits requires learning (see Griffiths et al. 2009; Mallon & Weinberg 2006; Samuels 2002).

there a specific type or set of mental processes—or perhaps even specific neural substrates—uniquely involved in moral experiences and computation?[4] Is moral cognition universal, ancient, innate, functionally and domain-specific?

Answering whether morality is an adaptation is a complex task, and significant disagreement among scholars persists on this issue. Further complexity is added, of course, by the problem of unequivocally defining conceptually what morality and moral cognition are—even before attempting to empirically identify how they manifest and where they might be located in the brain (Young & Dungan 2012). It is, in fact, far from clear whether it is possible to define morality and moral cognition as unified, consistent, and universal phenomena and objects of inquiry (see e.g., Goodwin 2017; Hindriks & Sauer 2020; Parkinson et al. 2011; Sinnott-Armstrong & Wheatley 2014; Stitch 2019). Addressing these issues is highly relevant for the current purposes, as the inability to affirm the existence of a specifically moral kind of cognition, or to provide a clear functionalist-adaptationist explanation and definition of morality, would render the idea that human moral cognition and morality are naturally constrained by their evolutionary history untenable.

A relatively non-controversial starting point to understand what moral cognition might be—in order to assess whether and how it evolved—is to treat it as a peculiar kind of *normative* cognition. Empirical evidence, evolutionary models and theoretical research seem to converge on the idea that normative cognition can be legitimately considered an adaptation. Why?

First, the function of 'general' normative cognition seems relatively straightforward and less controversial. Normative cognition consists in the regulation of one's and others' conduct to maintain norm-conformity, by proscribing and prescribing types of actions, and regulating sanctions and punishment for free-riders (Birch 2021; Kumar & Campbell 2022, chapter 3). So conceived, norm-

---

4   See Arvan (2021, 96-99), Greene & Young (2020), Han (2017), Pascual et al. (2013), Young & Dungan (2012) for some reviews of experimental findings about the neural correlates of moral cognition.

compliance and the disposition to punish defectors are psychological traits that evolved because they favored and stabilized cooperation and cultural transmission (Birch 2021; Boyd & Richerson 1992; Kumar & Campbell 2022; Machery & Mallon 2010). Birch (2021) identifies three core elements of normative cognition: (i) the detection or prediction of failures in norm-compliance (both by others and oneself); (ii) the activation of emotional and motivational pressure (e.g., anger, shame, uneasiness) to anticipate or intervene on failures in norm-compliance; (iii) the activation of solution strategies to restore conformity (by correcting one's or others' behavior, asking for forgiveness, or punishing).

Second, although it is not easy to ascertain how ancient the appearance of normative cognition and behavior may be, norms and normative cognition seem to be ubiquitous in human societies and to have emerged very early in their evolutionary history (Kumar & Campbell, 2022; Machery & Mallon 2010). Andrews (2020) suggests that some basic forms of normative cognition and behavior can be found not only in the great apes, but also in other non-human animals (especially mammals) who are able to distinguish (a) agential vs. non-agential violations of norms, (b) in-group vs. out-group normal behavior (choosing to follow what the majority of one's group does), and (c) negatively reacting in front of others' violations of norms and implementing corrective strategies (see also Ross 2018).

Third, paradigmatic experimental studies report that a distinctive, domain-specific capacity to detect cheaters and norm violations meets the remaining aforementioned conditions for considering an evolved capacity an adaptation (Cosmides & Tooby 2005; Cummins 1996b; Machery & Mallon 2010). In particular, these studies show that both adults and very young children perform significantly better in reasoning tasks that involve the violation of *deontic* conditionals such as "if X is here, then Y *must be* there" than in tasks involving *indicative* conditionals such as "if A is here, then B *is* there" (see Cummins 1996a; 1996b; Harris & Núñez 1996).

Nonetheless, we might doubt that the cognitive processes at play in an alleged *specifically moral* kind of cognition are the same as those at play in any other kind of normative cognition. There are in fact several kinds of norms to which we (reasonably) do not refer as 'moral', and others that are not morally relevant at all.[5] Although several psychological traits involved in moral cognition *as in other domains*—like norm-based cognition and emotions— can be legitimately considered evolutionary adaptations, the idea that a specific capacity for moral cognition was *directly* selected by evolution is not supported by available research and evidence (Arvan 2021; Machery & Mallon 2010). If we consider the aforementioned indicators to hold a capacity an evolutionary adaptation—functional specificity, universality, antiquity, innateness –, none of them seems to be clearly present in the case of moral cognition.

Unclear and contingent function. Although many functionalist-adaptationist accounts of moral cognition and morality have been defended in recent years (Casebeer 2003; Cosmides & Tooby 1992; Curry 2016; de Waal 2006; Dennett 2003; Joyce 2006; Kitcher 2011; Luco 2014; 2019; Rai & Fiske 2011; Sinclair 2012; Tomasello & Vaish 2013), the task of identifying the biological-evolutionary function of morality and of a specific kind of cognition dedicated to morality is particularly problematic (Buchanan & Powell 2015; 2018, 79-91 and 387-388; Smyth 2017).

The most common view among adaptationist accounts is to conceive of the main function of morality and moral cognition as that of reducing social conflicts by fostering cooperation and social cohesion and, according to some, even increasing well-being and its equal distribution (Boehm 2012; Luco 2019; Railton 1986). Intuitively, this view makes sense. Moral institutions (e.g., systems of moral norms) may have been useful for dealing with several socio-environmental needs and challenges over the course of evolution, and cognitive traits involved in moral thinking and reasoning might have been selected because they contributed to benefit both individuals and groups who displayed them (Baumard et al. 2013; Boehm 2012;

---

5   Other, non-moral (or only indirectly morally relevant) kinds of normativity may concern: logical consistency and/or rationality (e.g., "given p, you should/shouldn't conclude/believe that q"), aesthetics ("never wear plaid and stripes together"), prudence ("if you want to be healthy, you should eat better/do sports"), or conventions ("you should always leave a tip here").

Buchanan 2020, 138-142, 152-153; Campbell & Kumar 2012; Campbell & Woodrow 2003, 361-371; Luco 2019; Stanford 2018, 11, 19-20). However, to reduce moral cognition and morality to the overly simplified functions that adaptationist accounts usually refer to—e.g., enhancing cooperation, reducing social tensions, promoting well-being—seems incorrect for several reasons.[6]

First, if to endorse a functionalist-adaptationist account of moral cognition and morality means to state that the function they perform now is the same one for which they have been selected over the course of evolution, this claim is both epistemically unjustified (Godfrey-Smith 1994; Smyth 2017) and empirically false. As far as the empirical plausibility of these views is concerned, recent historical trends, cross-cultural empirical research, and comparative ethnological studies show that different environmental, social, and epistemic conditions predict not only change in moral institutions, norms, and collective practices, but also in individuals' psychological capacities involved in moral reasoning and deliberation, sensitivity, and behavior, highlighting the extraordinary plasticity of humans' psychological outlook (Buchanan & Powell 2018; Kumar & Campbell 2022; see also Reger et al. 2018; Stoks et al. 2016; Watkins 2021, for adaptive plasticity in non-human species). Specifically, a substantial body of empirical data shows that humans can reason, feel, and act in ways that significantly deviate from what would be prescribed by biological and socio-cultural 'functional' normativity, depending on socio-ecological circumstances (Buchanan & Powell 2015; 2018; Henrich 2020; Welzel 2013; Inglehart 2018).

---

6   An 'indirect' reason for why morality and moral cognition might not have (had) the function of enhancing cooperation, social cohesion, and prosperity that many scholars attribute to them is that there are many, stronger alternative explanatory hypotheses for the higher levels of cooperation, cohesion, and prosperity that several human societies experienced in recent history. Progressively increasing levels of well-being and social cohesion, for instance, strongly correlate with progressive increase in the political and repressive power of States and legal institutions (Runge 1984), as well as with the development of market institutions and the spread of capitalism (more on this below).

Therefore, our understanding of the function of morality and moral cognition can vary depending on the environments and normative standards that emerge in response to different environmental cues. In fact, there are no 'absolute' or 'intrinsic' functions, i.e., existing independently of the larger system of which the entity in question is a part; functions always depend on systemic-ecological circumstances, and vary when these conditions change (Smyth 2017, 1131-32).

As other biological traits, institutions, or artifacts, certain cognitive traits and moral institutions can be considered more functional in some circumstances than in others, and different socio-environmental conditions can radically alter what is more useful, efficient, or appropriate to assess specific environmental problems, even by altering phenotypical characteristics in a relatively short time.

Although the function of moral cognition and morality appears to be more complex, contextual, and historically variable than many evolutionary psychologists have claimed, some scholars emphasize that several elements of the ancestral conditions in which proto-morality and moral cognition evolved are still present in contemporary societies (Greene 2013; Kitcher 2011). Philip Kitcher, for instance, conceives of "the current human situation as analogous to that initially prompting the ethical project. As it was in the beginning, so too now—for the conflicts to which our ancestors' lives were subject are mirrored in contemporary hostilities across the human population" (Kitcher 2011, 8). According to Kitcher, moral cognition and morality still perform the same evolutionary function for which they were selected. This is, however, only partly true. As I will argue more thoroughly in the following sections, humans have developed social practices, institutions, cognitive abilities, and dispositions that completely disrupted the socio-ecological circumstances in which—according to several prominent scholars—morality and moral cognition were selected because of their fitness-enhancing contribution. In turn, morality and moral cognition's function—assuming that we can identify one—may have changed as well (Smyth 2017).

As emphasized by Nicholas Smyth (2017), functions are highly sensitive to environmental changes: nothing has an intrinsic function—that is, a role perfomed independently of the properties of the broader system to which it belongs. For example, the white fur of the polar bear serves a camouflaging function, but only because the bear's environment is white. The color of the polar bear's environment is thus an enabling condition for that function: researchers hypothesize that around 600,000 years ago a species of bears with darker fur moved towards the Arctic Circle, and the color of the Arctic environment enabled those individuals born with lighter fur to live longer and leave more descendants (Kurtén 1964). Today, conclusions can be drawn about the current function of the polar bear's light fur because the enabling conditions for its current function are the same as those that explain why the light fur of the bears was adaptive in the past. However, Smyth suggests, let us imagine that a population of polar bears is transferred to the Amazon rainforest, where such conditions do not exist (or, in a sadly more plausible scenario, that their habitat ceases to be predominantly white, as is actually happening due to global warming). In that case, would the polar bear's white fur be misfunctioning, have lost its function, or simply be unable to perform it? If many generations of polar bears maintained their white fur in non-white environments, it seems that etiological theories of function would have to conclude that the fur has lost its original function, as the trait no longer produces the effect for which it was selected, yet it persists.

What about the current environmental and social conditions that made moral (cognitive and institutional) responses adaptive for most of our species' evolutionary history (and perhaps even before, for our non-human ancestors)? Many scholars emphasize that today's world is, for most human societies (albeit with significant differences), markedly different from the EEA in which humans have lived for most of their history. Evolutionary psychologists claim that this environment was characterized by small societies of 50-150 individuals, strong familiar and community ties, repeated interactions with the same people, harsh resource scarcity, existential threats from pathogens and predators, and constant intergroup conflicts. But over the last millennia, and even more drastically in the past few centuries and decades, humans have created technologies, practices, and institutions that had never been seen before on Earth, dramatically altering and almost completely erasing the enabling conditions that, according to functionalist-adaptationist theories of morality *à la* Kitcher (2011), Haidt (2012), Joyce (2006) and many others would explain the emergence of human morality and define both its original and current function.

Smyth (2017) notes that a feature of modern and contemporary societies (particularly WEIRD ones) appears to be that the enabling conditions for the cooperative function of the 'moral' responses developed by *homo sapiens* have not only been reduced or erased, but even reversed compared to pre-modern societies. As Adam Smith (1776) already observed two hundred and fifty years ago, modern forms of economic exchange create the conditions for individualism and self-interest to contribute to the stability of social groups by promoting mutually beneficial competition (not cooperation), increasing the availability of goods. It is true that, in tight-knit social contexts such as hunter-gatherer communities and agrarian societies preceding the advent of industrialization and capitalism, selfishness and other less cooperative traits towards the members of one's own tribe and social group could have had disastrous effects on cooperation, social cohesion and well-being. But as Mandeville (1714) already noted, traits that were dangerous in pre-modern societies can lead to individual and collective benefits in radically different contexts, such as those characterizing modern and contemporary societies. This does not mean claiming that societies have become more selfish (not at all, as we will see) nor does it imply an apology for the greater selfishness of people living in contemporary capitalist and consumerist societies. Smyth's example serves to show that, even for contingent and unintended reasons, societies can change so significantly that psychological traits that were once non-adaptive become adaptive, and traits that were once adaptive become maladaptive (Smyth 2017).

There are, moreover, alternative hypotheses that appear more convincing and dynamics that appear more relevant for explaining the increase in cooperation, social cohesion, existential security, and the reduction of conflict and violence in contemporary societies that do not seem to depend on the idea— as Kitcher hypothesizes—that morality continues to perform its original function (in a better or enhanced way). First, Smyth suggests, increase in social cohesion and decrease in violence in recent history (cf. Pinker 2011) correlate with the rise of state power. At no point in human history have states been able to identify, stop, and punish criminals as effectively as now, far more effectively than morality alone could. Second, it is plausible that greater cooperation, inclusivity, prosperity, well-being, and security are the result of industrial capitalism and technological development, rather than ancestral traits continuing to perform their conflict-resolution and cooperation-enhancing functions in response to problems that are similar to those faced by our ancestors (for some, the current function of capitalism is precisely to produce greater well-being and the mutually beneficial social cohesion that results from it; see Runge 1984).

Conversely, morality may even have negative effects on social cohesion, political stability, and economic development (Stehr 2006, 123-135). Moral language is often used in ways—such as moral denigration and grandstanding (Tosi & Warmke 2016; 2020a; 2020b)—that, rather than promoting cooperation, can hinder it, e.g., by fueling polarization, conflict, and even violence between individuals and groups (Arvan 2019). Many pointed out that moralization has significant and problematic effects on contemporary politics. The United States in the past decades has become emblematic of a polarized and tribalistic (even Manichean) political culture (Haidt 2012): We, and those who think like Us, are the good ones; while They, those who think differently, are the bad, ignorant, corrupt, and perverse ones. If this is the case, then the idea that morality still performs the evolutionary function for which it was selected might need to be reconsidered. The 'morality' that once facilitated cooperation in the Pleistocene no longer seems to increase cooperation today: rather, it makes it more difficult. Perhaps to perform that same function, we would need to be less moral, more moral, or moral in a different way. The adaptationist view of morality itself seems to point in this direction: consider social discounting and hostility (often implicit) towards different ethnic groups; the difficulty of representing and caring about the condition of large numbers of people (scope neglect); or the tendency to prefer what is near in space and time (proximity bias, social and temporal discounting). Are these traits, likely adaptive in the EEA and still largely characterizing human morality, continuing to serve the function of enhancing cooperation?

The idea that the psychology, institutions, and moral beliefs that evolved in response to fundamental socio-environmental challenges for the survival of *Homo sapiens* over tens of thousands of years no longer serve the same function of promoting cooperation as they once did must be taken seriously (Greene 2013; Singer 2005); what we consider 'moral' today may not necessarily be linked to fulfilling a specific evolutionary function. In the following, we will analyze this possibility in greater detail.

The fact that ecological conditions can change even drastically may constitute a serious problem if our moral cognition was actually rigidly fixed to its original ancestral configurations, and unable to face the challenges that new environmental conditions require (recall Persson & Savulescu and Pinker's claims about evolutionary mismatch quoted above). As I will stress later, however, this does not appear to be the case. As neuroscientist and philosopher Joshua Greene and other scholars have recently highlighted (e.g., Singer 2005; 2011), in fact, only certain aspects of our moral psychology (type-1, or *model-free* cognitive processes) seem to be more directly explainable evolutionarily by reference to their etiology and learning history (not only phylogenetic, but also ontogenetic; not only 'natural', but also cultural), and for this reason they are often more inflexible and harder to control and modify (Cushman 2013; Greene 2017). However, other cognitive mechanisms and capacities involved in moral (as in non-moral) learning and decision-making (type-2, or *model-based* cognitive processes) are significantly more flexible and amenable to evidence and to conscious and critical scrutiny. Relying more on the latter rather than on the former might help us better address new and more complex moral problems (Bina 2022; Bina et al. 2024; Greene 2013; 2014; 2017; Singer 2005; 2011); and even judgements based on model-free intuitions can change if there are new learning opportunities of the right kind.

Universality. Conceiving moral cognition and morality as universal is also problematic. Of course, this judgment strongly depends on our definition/conception of morality. But although evidence and theoretical models support the idea that norms and normative cognition are likely present in every human society and culture, it is not equally clear whether *moral* norms and cognition are also universal, even if we assume a very minimal definition of moral cognition (see Joyce 2006, 70–71; Railton 2017, 173).[7]

Oldness. Considering the above, it seems implausible also to maintain that moral cognition and morality are evolutionarily ancient, both if we look at the history of humanity and at the cognitive and behavioral traits of our non-human ancestors. Some aspects of human cognition involved in moral judgements and behavior are certainly present in our non-human relatives (Brosnan 2006; Brosnan & de Waal 2003; de Waal 1996). However, without denying any biological continuity nor conceiving human capacities as 'privileged' or 'superior', many comparable cognitive skills and institutions cannot be found in our non-human ancestors (Bowles & Gintis 2013; Henrich 2015; Machery & Mallon 2010, 5-10; Prinz 2008, 397-402; Ross 2018; Korsgaard 2006). Moreover, as we will see more in detail in the next sections, cross-cultural and historical evidence shows that several cognitive traits and configurations of moral institutions appeared in the history of human societies only recently (Buchanan & Powell 2015; 2018; Henrich 2020; Kumar & Campbell 2022; Pinker 2011; Schulz et al. 2019).

Innateness, domain-specificity, and the moral-conventional distinction. The existence of an innate, domain-specific capacity for moral cognition has been widely questioned in recent years. In the past decades, several scholars have defended the idea that humans might have an innate capacity to distinguish moral norms from non-moral ones (e.g., Dwyer et al. 2010; Hauser 2006; Joyce 2006), especially in light of influential studies on the 'moral-conventional distinction' in young children (Smetana 1981; Turiel

---

7   For more on this point, see Machery & Mallon (2010). As the authors point out, "the universality of norms should not be confused with the universality of moral norms" (31). See also Stich (2019).

1983; for a review, see Machery & Stich 2022). According to this fortunate paradigm, evidence shows that young children cross-culturally distinguish between norms that are seen as independent from authority, universally applicable, and justifiable by reference to harms and rights (*moral* norms), and norms that depend on authority and/or contextual contingencies, and whose violations are judged less seriously (*conventional* norms). According to this distinction, for example, it is *morally* unacceptable to hit people for fun, but it is only *conventionally* unacceptable to go to school or the office wearing flip-flops or pajamas. The ability of children to distinguish between these norms very early in life has been judged by many as a strong evidence of the innateness of a peculiar kind of normative cognition, i.e., *moral* cognition. This conclusion is based on a 'poverty-of-the-stimulus' argument: such a universal sensitivity to the moral-conventional distinction emerges so early in life that it cannot depend on the development of other cognitive skills. This suggests that it might be unlearned, i.e., innate (Mikhail 2007).[8]

However, several scholars pointed out that empirical evidence is far from supporting this conclusion (Kelly et al. 2007; Machery & Stich 2022; Machery & Mallon 2010; Sinnott-Armstrong & Wheatley 2014; Stich 2019; Young & Dungan 2012). First, other classic studies on the moral-conventional distinction in young children show that kids almost never conceive of social norms as genuinely 'conventional' (Shweder et al. 1987; Gabennesch 1990). Second, the idea that moral and conventional rules are clearly distinguishable according to the aforementioned criteria of authority-dependence, scope of validity/applicability, harm-sensitivity, and seriousness of violations contrasts with empirical evidence. First, these features often do not co-occur; we can list infinite cases of moral and conventional norms that do not meet one or more of the aforementioned criteria (Stich 2019). For example, violations of norms that are often considered moral can be less serious than

---

8   The poverty of the stimulus argument was originally formulated by Chomsky (1975) to explain the capacity to speak virtually any possible language just being exposed to a few (insufficient) environmental stimuli, before and independently of the development of other cognitive traits.

conventional ones. Breaking the promise not to eat the last slice of a cake at home or telling a white lie seem to be violations of the former case, but they are typically judged less seriously than, e.g., going to work naked or continuously interrupting a seminar without raising one's hand. Or consider the norm according to which nobody should eat putrefying meat. This norm appears to be authority-independent, universal, harm-sensitive and serious, but it does not appear to be a moral rule. Furthermore, several studies in social psychology (Cushman et al. 2012; Haidt et al. 1993) report that people judge fake or victimless actions[9] as seriously wrong and authority-independent, but but they do not justify their moral judgements by referring to harms, rights, or empathic concern for the subjects involved—since there are actually no victims nor harms involved (for further examples and discussion, see Prinz 2008, 384-385; Machery & Stich 2022; Machery & Mallon 2010, 33-35; Stich 2019).[10]

As Machery and Mallon point out,

> while many philosophers, psychologists, and anthropologists have claimed that morality is a product of the evolution of the human species, the evidence for this claim is weak at best. First, we do not know whether moral norms are present in every culture: because researchers endorse rich characterizations of what moral norms are, it is not obvious that norms that have the distinctive properties of moral norms will be found in every culture, and, in any case, researchers have simply not shown that, in numerous cultures, there are norms that fit some rich characterization of moral norms. Second, the claim that early on children display some complex moral knowledge in spite of variable and impoverished environmental stimuli is based on the research on the moral/conventional distinction. Although this research remains widely accepted in much of psychology, a growing body of evidence has highlighted its shortcomings. Third, the other pieces of evidence often cited in the literature on the evolution of morality do not constitute evidence that moral norms and moral judgments, understood

---

9   Such as masturbating with a dead chicken or cleaning the toilet with one's national flag (see Haidt 1993; 2012).

10   Note that, while there might be borderline cases, these are not conclusive reasons to abandon a conceptual distinction between moral and conventional norms.

as a specific type of norms and normative judgments, evolved, rather than evidence that normative cognition evolved (2010, 35).[11]

Genetic heritability, culture and cognitive-behavioral development. The idea that individual cognitive development can be conceived as rigidly genetically pre-programmed is also scientifically incorrect. Recent research in behavioral genetics and cultural evolution emphasizes that genetic expression and individual cognitive and behavioral development critically depend on interactions between genes and multiple environmental, social and cultural factors (Henrich 2015; Kumar & Campbell 2022; Stotz 2014; Schulz 2020; Sterelny 2012; Uchiyama et al. 2021). There are indeed good reasons to "reject the predeterministic and instructionist frameworks common to contemporary evolutionary psychology and other gene-centered perspectives on human behavior" (Lickliter & Honeycutt 2003).

Therefore, understanding moral cognition and morality as evolutionary adaptations appears problematic. Can neuroscientific research offer relevant insights on this issue? Is there any neuro-cognitive mechanism specifically dedicated to moral experiences (a 'moral brain') that can be isolated from, for instance, mechanisms involved in other related kinds of computation and experience—such as emotions, empathy, social cognition, norm cognition, cost-benefit analysis, prudential reasoning? Recent neuroscientific evidence shows that the main neural correlates of moral judgment and decision-making recruit several brain systems and pathways involved in many non-specifically moral (i.e., domain-general) activities, such as emotional processing, social cognition, valuation, counterfactual reasoning, agency, cognitive control, planning, mental time-travel, prudential reasoning, and more (Arvan 2021; Borg et al. 2006; Cushman 2008; Gray & Wegner 2009; Greene et al. 2004; Kennett & Matthews 2009; Paxton et al. 2012; Shenhav & Greene 2010; Waytz et al. 2010). None of these capacities, however, is specifically or uniquely involved in moral cognition. Basically,

---

11   For another skeptical view on moral nativism, see Sterelny (2010).

it seems that "moral neuroscience has provided no candidates for substrates or systems dedicated to moral cognition [...] So far, the uniquely moral brain has appeared nowhere—perhaps because it does not exist" (Young & Dungan 2012, 5-7).

On the contrary, moral cognition, practices and institutions seem to involve and critically depend on the development and use of several adaptive cognitive traits (Ayala 2010; Nichols 2004; Prinz 2008), but none of them is "distinctly 'moral' or inherently conducive to social cooperation. [...] [T]hey were each plausibly selected in evolutionary history for amoral reasons: as capacities that enable fitness advantages irrespective of whether they are used to general moral actions conducive to social cooperation. [...] [M] oral cognition is almost certainly not a biological adaptation for social cooperation" (Arvan 2021, 99).

In this section, I sought to address a first aspect of the hard-wiring thesis—the idea that moral cognition and morality are bound by the reasons for which they were selected in the EEA. In particular, I challenged the idea that morality and moral cognition can be conceived as universal and domain-specific sets of cognitive-behavioral traits dedicated to perform specific evolutionary functions. The idea that specifically moral cognitive traits evolved in a way that makes them hard to modify nowadays—because they are still doomed to perform their original, ancestral biological function—appears problematic. The points just made provide preliminary reasons to cast doubt on the soundness of the hard-wiring thesis.

A second possibility is to consider human moral capacities as evolutionary by-products, rather than adaptations. What if morality, rather than being a direct product of natural selection, were a by-product of other cognitive and social traits (which were directly selected for their fitness-enhancing contribution)? Although prominent contributors to this debate have rejected this hypothesis (see Buchanan & Powell 2015; Machery & Mallon 2010, 23), this view appears significantly less problematic the adaptationist one. I address this problem in chapter 5. Before doing that, let us examine some additional empirical objections to the hard-wiring thesis.

3.2 *Environment of Evolutionary Adaptedness: Population size, intergroup contact and hostility*

The hard-wiring thesis is grounded on empirical assumptions concerning features of human populations and other socio-ecological conditions and challenges in the EEA. Several scholars have inferred from paleoanthropological records and recent socio-psychological research that the cognitive and motivational shortcomings human beings widely display nowadays are the direct product of selective pressures in ancestral environments. These pressures rewarded and favored the transmission of traits and responses that were advantageous in small societies of hunters and gatherers: "these limitations are the result of the evolutionary function of morality being to maximize the fitness of small cooperative groups competing for resources" (Persson & Savulescu 2017, 286; see also Greene 2013, 23). A passage from Buchanan and Powell (2015) portrays this view clearly:

> Examinations of the ethnographic and archeological records attest to the extant and prehistorical ubiquity of intergroup conflict, and there is strong evidence that core elements of human moral psychology were forged in conflict between large ethnolinguistic groups. "Parochial altruism", which consists in the combination of in-group favoritism/ empathy and out-group antagonism/antipathy, is among the most cross-culturally robust features of human moral psychology and a direct prediction of group selectionist accounts of morality. A striking feature of the received selectionist explanation, therefore, is that it implies morality is essentially an intragroup affair. The same ecological conditions and selection pressures that made moral traits adaptive would have imposed a fitness cost on extending "evolutionarily excessive" moral consideration to out-group members. Just as free-riding on in-group members will tend to undermine group performance in a competitive intergroup arena, so too will excessive moral consideration toward members of the out-group. The selectively optimal combination appears to have been reasonably expansive moral consideration toward members of one's in-group (with a caveat for gender), and highly strategic—including predatory, antagonistic, and apathetic—behavior toward strang-ers, who were often distrusted, dehumanized, and delegitimized (Buchanan & Powell 2015, 42).

In this section, I unpack this view into three empirical sub-claims and seek to assess their validity.

i. Population size and interactions. Human communities have been small and relatively homogeneous (both genetically and culturally) for most of *homo sapiens'* history. Also, available technologies in the EEA allowed limited interactions between individuals and groups (e.g., with geographically, cutlurally, and genetically distant ones). Chances to harm, benefit, cooperate with, and to morally consider distant and diverse subjects and events have been extremely low for hundreds of thousands of years (Greene 2007; Persson & Savulescu 2012; 2017; Singer 2005). Imagination, anticipation and evaluation of consequences, caring about and investing in cooperative relationships with faraway and/or culturally diverse individuals, deviating from local moral and social norms are all costly behaviors; for thousands of years they have been extremely much more costly than today, and there is no reason why bio-cultural selective pressures should have selected ultra-inclusivist, open-minded, and farsighted psychological traits. If the etiological theory of function introduced above is plausible, this is why humans' cognitive, moral, and prosocial traits are still very biased and limited in scope nowadays.

ii. Tribalism and hostility. In recent decades, research and discussion across various disciplines have emphasized that human cognition is strongly, rigidly, and universally biased towards in-group favoritism and discrimination against out-groups. According to some studies, such differences in attitudes and beliefs about in-groups and out-groups are often attributed to 'social discounting' (people simply care more about kin and less about strangers). However, these traits are frequently associated with intolerance, disgust, contempt, xenophobia, direct hostility, and even aggression (Choi & Bowles 2007; De Dreu et al. 2022; Kumar & Campbell 2022; Lee 2016; Wrangham & Peterson 1996).

iii. Selective advantage of limited cognition and prosociality. Limits to imaginative and decisional capacities, to expanded and impersonal prosociality, and to inclusivist and universalist moralities—along with cognitive biases, conformism, parochial altruism, in-group favoritism, scope neglect, discrimination, and hostility—have been selected because they were adaptive for thousands of years in pre-modern societies. These traits enhanced fitness either by being more efficient than costlier traits, such as indiscriminate prosociality, or by directly protecting individuals from various existential threats (Aarøe et al. 2017; Bennis et al. 2010; Faulkner et al. 2004; Haselton & Nettle 2006; Kurzban & Leary 2001; Navarrete & Fessler 2006; Neuberg & Schaller 2016; Oaten et al. 2011; Page 2022; Tomasello 2016). On the contrary, more farsighted, open-minded, inclusivist, and prosocial traits— such as extended intergroup trust and cooperation, openness to new experiences, and adaptability to change—were not selected because they proved to be more costly than beneficial. Ultra-cooperative, adventurous, and farsighted traits did not survive, reproduce, or spread as effectively as moderately cooperative, conformist, and shortsighted cognitive and behavioral traits. In what follows, I show that recent research suggests these three main claims lack empirical support.

Counterevidence

i. First, paleoanthropological evidence suggests that early human societies were not as small and close-knit as many scholars portray them. Archaeological records indicate that human communities have been composed of thousands of individuals for at least the past 50,000 years (Richerson & Boyd 1999; Sterelny 2019)—figures far exceeding the small groups of 50 to 150 individuals frequently cited in the literature (Dunbar 1993; 2010; Persson & Savulescu 2012). Even contemporary hunter-gatherer communities—such as the Martu from the Western Australian desert, or the !Kung San people from Western Kalahari—stably coexist and cooperate with groups of thousands of people (Richerson & Boyd 1999, 254). Recent evidence about social networks and interactions between residential units in contemporary hunting and gathering communities shows that these societies are organized in large groups of thousands of individuals; and that residency, group membership, and social interactions are much more fluid and dynamic than previously thought, approaching the numbers of modern communities based on agriculture and industry (Bird et al. 2019; Segovia-Cuéllar & Del Savio 2021).

ii. As already suggested by Allport (1954), recent anthropological studies on intergroup relations have questioned the link between in-group favoritism and hostility towards out-groups, showing that no empirical support exists for this correlation (Corr et al. 2015; Yamagishi & Mifune 2016), both among humans and non-human primates (Brewer 1999; Pisor & Surbeck 2019). Moreover, recent research in evolutionary biology and anthropology also investigated incentives for tolerance, disincentives for violence, and opportunities for encounters between groups of conspecifics in primates, including early humans. Contrary to the view that human psychology is essentially biased towards in-group favoritism and out-group discrimination (and even hostility), these findings suggest that highly cooperative and tolerant attitudes and behaviors towards strangers were already present in early human societies, as well as in the social behavior of our closest primate relatives (Pisor & Surbeck 2019).

As Kim Sterelny observes,

> (i) there is no clear signature of collective violence on human remains until the very end of the Pleistocene. (ii) There are no battle or raiding scenes in Pleistocene cave art. (iii) The development of projectile weapons, and the associated abilities to stalk and to lie in ambush make chimp-style raids and patrols dangerous, in ways it is not for chimps. (iv) In contrast to skeletal evidence from early farmers, there is little evidence that Pleistocene foragers were routinely resource stressed; that they lived in regimes of near-starvation that compelled a struggle for resources. (v) Jointly, these facts about risks and resource availability suggest that the cost/benefit balance would often favour fairly peaceable relations with neighbours. That is especially true because there are positive benefits from peace […] forager ethnography certainly shows that while foragers are capable of war, they are also capable of peace (Sterelny 2019, 208).

This should not, of course, lead us to conclude that biased traits such as parochial altruism and intergroup hostility were absent in early human societies (they were, and they are still present nowadays).[12] However, the fact that significant levels of tolerance and cooperation between strangers have been also present for millennia in human societies suggests that human cognition should not be seen as so rigidly bound to a bellicose and tribal destiny as many have recently argued in light of *ad hoc* descriptions of ancestral environments. On the contrary, a more complex picture of intergroup interactions in early humans suggests that intergroup cognition and behavior can be significantly more flexible than the hard-wiring thesis states (on this point, see also Buchanan 2020). Recent research in evolutionary anthropology challenges the idea that parochial and exclusive psychological traits dominated the history of human societies for millennia, showing that more prosocial, tolerant, inclusive cooperative traits could also have evolved. But how, and why?

iii. In the previous sections, we examined a core claim commonly defended by advocates of the hard-wiring thesis: on the one hand, limited prosocial (and even hostile) cognitive and behavioral traits have been selected because they were adaptive (i.e., fitness-enhancing because efficient and functional in facing existential threats and opportunities in the EEA). On the other hand, more inclusivist, tolerant, reflective, far-sighted, and open-minded traits would have been comparatively much more costly and inefficient for most of our evolutionary history (Haselton & Nettle 2006; Tomasello 2016). However, this claim appears to conflict with both available evidence and theoretical models in evolutionary anthropology. For instance, paleoanthropological data suggest that tolerance, cooperation and inclusiveness beyond one's narrow social group were present in the EEA, and empirical research shows that these traits are vastly more present nowadays (although

---

12 Sterelny notes that "while sceptical of the view that hostility was the default [...] in the Pleistocene, the distinction between one-of-us and not one-of-us certainly mattered enormously. I would be astounded if there was anything like an attitude of default trust towards members of out-groups" (2019, 208). However, note that while life in the Pleistocene was probably not dominated by starvation and inter-group conflict, according to forager ethnographic records, hostility and conflict *within* groups were likely quite high (Boehm 2012).

clearly not universal). Might they have technically 'evolved' as well? If so, how can we explain the presence of costly cooperative, inclusivist, and reflective traits in human psychology, behavior and social institutions?

As observed above, traits can evolve—i.e., change and spread in populations of organisms—through various evolutionary mechanisms: natural selection is not the only one (Gould & Lewontin 1979). We also noted that the idea of a specific cognitive system dedicated to morality as an adaptation faces several difficulties. Nonetheless, we might hypothesize that reflective and prosocial traits not specific to the moral domain evolved in adaptationist terms. Traits favoring more inclusive prosocial dispositions, trust, and impartial concern for the interests of out-group individuals might have been selected because they conferred several direct advantages to the individuals and groups exhibiting them. These advantages could include increased opportunities for broader systems of direct or indirect reciprocity, sharing essential material and epistemic resources, giving birth to stronger offspring through intergroup mating, and so forth.

As Sauer correctly notices,

> a cultural-learning account of evolution can explain why in a highly cooperative niche (i.e., increasingly large communities such as cities), there are adaptive advantages to people having a non-discriminating disposition to cooperate even with strangers and outgroup members (because of rewards from trade or information transmission). The next generation of norm learners [...] then acquires this set of undiscriminating norms of cooperation from the previous generation, such that at the end of this process, we have people acting on the simple norm of "be nice to people in general" (Sauer 2023, 39).

Paleoanthropological evidence suggests that, like their nonhuman relatives and ancestors, early humans began associating with out-group strangers very early in the history of our species. Primarily driven by incentives to acquire useful information—such as strategies to cope with common environmental challenges— intergroup contacts not only increased the risk of threats and danger but also enhanced reproductive fitness for individuals who engaged openly and peacefully in new social exchanges. For instance, these interactions often led to increased knowledge about obtaining or producing food, tools, and shelters (see Pisor & Surbeck 2019). Hence, cooperative and tolerant traits in intergroup social exchanges might have been selected as they proved highly beneficial in contexts where greater division of labor between neighboring communities was required (Krebs 2011, 180; Tomasello 2016; see also Buchanan 2020, 152-153).

Furthermore, due to the increased opportunities for accessing highly beneficial resources created by intergroup interactions, humans who maintained fruitful relationships with out-group members significantly increased their reputation and status within their own social groups. Extra-community ties, in fact, can have (had) considerable beneficial effects not only for the individuals directly involved in those interactions but also for other members of their community and the group as a whole, thanks to the acquisition of more cost-effective skills and new empowering facilitated by intergroup and intercultural contact and exchange—a phenomenon also well-documented by sociological research in post-industrial societies (see Granovetter 1973).

As we will explore in greater detail in the next sections, as far as psychological change is concerned, the explanatory power of recent cultural evolutionary models appears significantly stronger than adaptationist hypotheses about the origins of morality and moral cognition. While overemphasizing the latter could lead one to accept the idea of a rigid, genetically predetermined, and universal moral-cognitive architecture, cultural evolutionary models are better equipped to explain the substantial psychological variations observed across societies and over time, offering both empirical evidence and robust theoretical foundations for the remarkable plasticity of human cognition and the flexibility and open-endedness of human morality.

4.

HISTORICAL AND CROSS-CULTURAL PSYCHOLOGICAL VARIATION

4.1. *Psychology as a historical science*

In the previous sections, I argued that the idea that the evolutionary history of our species selected a cognitive infrastructure that is (i) specifically designed for moral cognition and morality, and (ii) rigidly biased towards parochialism and exclusivity is problematic. On the contrary, increasing anthropological evidence and recent evolutionary models suggest that the main etiological, functionalist-adaptationist explanations of a hard-wired moral psychology are empirically inaccurate. As we have seen, the social, epistemic, and environmental conditions of the EEA were far more complex than the oversimplified accounts often presented in the literature. Furthermore, the core premise of classic evolutionary psychology, which conceives the EEA-Pleistocene as a privileged period in human evolution to explain current cognitive and behavioral traits, appears unjustified. If the main rationale beyond this view is that the late Pleistocene represents the epoch in which our species reached its current anatomical configuration, then this view relies on a form of neuro-anatomical reductionism and essentialism about human nature which is frankly untenable—especially given its stark contrast with historical and empirical evidence.

The idea that limited cognitive and behavioral traits, selected to address specific ecological challenges in the Pleistocene, remain widely present today because they are deeply embedded in our genes and brains, and insensitive to socio-cultural interventions and experiences appears to be scientifically poorly supported (see Buller 2006; Henrich 2020). After examining some empirical and theoretical shortcomings of the hard-wiring thesis, along with the assumptions and methods it relies upon, I will now turn to consider key pieces of counterevidence pointing in the opposite direction.

In this context, cultural evolutionary approaches to the study of human cognition and behavior provide compelling explanations for significant psychological variations across centuries, generations, and even within a single lifetime. It is important to emphasize that the link between socio-ecological enabling conditions and psychological or value shifts is not deterministic; however, scientific research can help identify associations and pathways that are more probable than others. A vast and still growing body of cross-cultural data shows substantial variations in people's psychological traits and moral values across different socio-cultural contexts, offering valuable evidence and insights into the drivers and dynamics underlying these changes.

What emerges from the growing body of cross-cultural empirical data on variations in human psychological traits and moral values collected in recent years is that there is essentially no universally shared moral cognition, since there is no universally shared human psychology or 'nature' in the first place (Prinz 2012). On the contrary, recent cultural evolutionary approaches emphasize the importance of understanding human psychology in more historical,[1] contextual, and anti-essentialist terms, as human cognitive and behavioral traits are profoundly influenced by the society and culture in which they develop (Muthukrishna et al. 2021; Henrich 2020).[2] Since human moral psychology appears to involve the interplay of several multi-purpose cognitive traits, I propose that the same cultural evolutionary approach be adopted to understand the ecological, social, and epistemic conditions that can enable (or prevent) the evolution of

---

1   To adopt a historical approach does not entail to fully abandon functionalist explanations; classic functionalist-adaptationist etiological explanations can also be considered 'historical'. A compelling synthesis between functionalist explanations of psychological-behavioral traits and the significant influence of culture—which can shape human cognition over much shorter timescales than classic evolutionary psychology typically acknowledges—can be found in Godfrey-Smith's *modern history*'s theory of functions: "the approach is historical because to ascribe a function is to make a claim about the past, but the relevant past is the recent past; modern history rather than ancient" (1994, 344).

2   According to Henrich, "You can't separate 'culture' from 'psychology' or 'psychology' from 'biology', because culture physically rewires our brains and thereby shapes how we think" (2020, 16-17).

moral systems as well as collective and individual psychological change.

Humans living in different societies vary considerably in their cognitive and behavioral traits. People from diverse cultures—both diachronically and synchronically—perceive, think and behave differently in terms of domain-general reasoning abilities, prosociality, trust, norms and conceptions of fairness (Henrich et al. 2001; Henrich 2020; Muthukrishna et al. 2020; Pinker 2011; Santos et al. 2017), moral judgments (Awad et al. 2019; Barrett et al. 2016; McNamara et al. 2019), moral emotions (Elison et al. 2005; Fessler 2004; Kumar & Campbell 2022; Prinz 2007; 2012; Wallbott & Scherer 1995), personality traits (Gurven et al. 2013; Smaldino et al. 2019), beliefs and behaviors concerning personal identity (Ma & Schoeneman 1997), and much more.[3]

Empirical research in cultural psychology and anthropology makes it possible to identify several conditions that predict significant psychological and value shifts extending far beyond the hard-wired tribalistic and shortsighted psychology that, according to classical evolutionary psychology and several contemporary commentators (Sauer 2019; 2023; Persson & Savulescu 2012; 2017) humans still universally carry with them since the Pleistocene. This body of evidence clearly shows that not only the *form* and *content* of human moralities (whether in theory, social practices, or institutions), but also human *psychology*—the way people think, perceive, and behave more broadly—can change substantially under different socio-ecological circumstances.[4] This evidence also strongly challenges the idea that moral change is only a matter of structural-institutional evolution that leverages or bypasses, a tribalistic, exclusivist, and myopic psychology presumed to be largely genetically determined and remains rigidly hard-wired into human brains. Cross-cultural evidence about the relations between different socio-cultural circumstances and psychological variations is extensive, and the trends I discuss here are not intended to

---

3   Different socio-cultural environments correlate with variations in psychological traits, skills, and dispositions even in domains that are not particularly morally relevant. See Henrich (2020, 38–41, 52-55).

4   This is probably the main difference between my view and Buchanan's (2020).

constitute an exhaustive review. Nonetheless, I hope that even a limited selection can illustrate that significant change beyond psychological tribalism, exclusiveness and myopia is empirically possible and well-documented by scientific data. Hopefully, greater understanding of the dynamics and enabling conditions of such changes will inform future moral and social change theories and strategies in a more realistic and constructive way.[5]

For reasons of space, I will focus on two main indicators of morally relevant psychological and behavioral variations: the increase and spread of *impersonal prosociality* and the rise of *emancipative values*. These notions refer to packages of psychological and behavioral traits that include, or strongly correlate with, among others, the following:

- Increased levels of trust, fairness, cooperation, generosity, and honesty towards strangers, anonymous people and institutions (including impersonal ones, such as governments);
- Reduced parochialism, in-group favoritism and loyalty;
- Endorsement of impartial, universalist, egalitarian and democratic moral principles, norms, and institutions;
- Preference for emancipative values over patriarchal ones;
- Lower levels of conformity and deference to tradition and authority;
- Higher levels of epistemic and behavioral self-regulation and control;
- Desire for and appreciation of decisional control and freedom of choice;
- Belief in free will and progress;
- Openness to change and new ideas;
- Increased propensity for analytical thinking;
- ...[6]

---

5   Let me emphasize once again that what I am going to report should not be understood as having intrinsic or direct ethical implications. Nonetheless, this does not mean that such evidence *cannot* have ethical implications. Reflecting on these implications, however, is not my main concern here.

6   I assume that all these psychological traits can be conceived as morally relevant in the sense that they matter for existing moral practices and challenges, and for our reflective understanding of them. Some of these

Empirical research documents significant differences in these indicators over time and across societies (Bond & Smith 1996; Henrich 2020; Inglehart 2018; Welzel 2013). Specifically, levels of impersonal prosociality and the endorsement of emancipative values are considerably higher in WEIRD societies according to several measures. WEIRD is a now classical acronym in the anthropological and psychological literature—standing for *Western, Educated, Industrialized, Rich* and *Democratic*—first introduced by Henrich and colleagues (2010). As Henrich repeatedly emphasizes in his work, from a global-historical point of view, WEIRD societies and psychology represent a very small minority, often situated at the extremes of the global distribution of psychological and behavioral traits (see Henrich 2020, 156-157). Cognitive and behavioral differences in the traits listed above correlate with diverse cultural and institutional backgrounds. This evidence supports the high flexibility of human psychology, and sheds light on conditions and dynamics underlying the directions and forms that it can assume. I will now briefly examine some recent data and hypotheses that seek to explain these psychological variations.

It is important to note tat a similar project aimed at understanding the fundamental dynamics regulating moral evolution from limited prosociality and parochial moralities to more complex, consistent, and inclusive moral systems—and even towards more "objective,

---

traits entail or relate to actual levels of altruistic motivation and behavior (e.g., dispositions to donate or to give up one's resources for the benefit of others), which can be measured using several paradigms in experimental economics and psychology. Other traits concern moral judgements more directly (e.g., what people explicitly judge to be right or wrong). Some traits may encompass both of these dimensions. *Impersonal trust*, for instance, can be assessed both via self-reported answers (e.g., to the Generalized Trust Question: "Generally speaking, would you say that most people can be trusted or that you can't be too careful in dealing with people?") and through classic experiments with economic games involving real money. Meta-analyses of experimental research on trust suggest that data from economic games and surveys using the GTQ are consistent (see Fehr et al. 2002; Johnson & Mislin 2011). For a more comprehensive overview of the many other cognitive and behavioral traits associated with impersonal prosociality, see Henrich (2020, 56).

impersonal, or agent-neutral reasons for action over subjective, personal, or agent relative reasons" (Jamieson 2002, 174) is not new. In the field of naturalistic moral philosophy, such a project was partially undertaken by Peter Singer in *The Expanding Circle* (1981/2011). However, this and other 20th-century theoretical attempts to account for significant moral change of this kind relied on far less rigorous scientific methodologies and more limited empirical evidence. Moreover, especially in the domain of ethics, theories of moral change have too often conflated descriptive-explanatory analysis of moral change with meta-ethical and normative considerations, inevitably muddying the waters of a scientific understanding of the real dynamics and conditions underlying moral change.

An exhaustive presentation and discussion of recent evidence on morally relevant psychological variations in different socio-ecological conditions would require more space. In what follows, I will focus on some of the main drivers that, according to recent evidence, have shifted the psychology of people living in certain socio-ecological conditions from being conformist, tribalistic, exclusivist, and myopic towards significantly higher levels of prosocial behavior, decisional autonomy, farsightedness, and other radical changes in their psychology and values.

4.2. *Evidence and explanations of robust psychological moral change*

Disruption of kin-based institutions. Our minds and behavior are to a significant extent influenced by the familiar contexts in which we grow up. Family is the first social reality that humans encounter when they come into the world, and in the vast majority of human societies it still constitutes the most fundamental institution regulating people's lives, shaping their cognitive and moral development (Sterelny 2010) and their values.

In contexts where social life is rigidly organized around intensive kin-based institutions, people's psychology—beliefs, motivations, emotions, perception—is shaped by the demands imposed by these strong relational ties. Norms of direct reciprocity and care, loyalty, obedience, respect for tradition and authority predominate; freedom, autonomy, openness to change and new experiences, trust in strangers and the creation of relational bonds outside one's close community and culture are discouraged and much more costly.

Historical, anthropological, and psychological data analyzed by Henrich and colleagues in the past few years document that psychological traits such as analytic skills, individualism, independence, and impersonal prosociality increase proportionally when the strength of intensive kin-based bonds and institutions decreases. Schulz and colleagues (2019) recently proposed the following hypothesis to explain the emergence of the unique psychological traits observed particularly in modern and contemporary WEIRD societies: by forbidding marriages between relatives (up to sixth cousins), the multiple bans and prescriptions that the Catholic Church of Rome began imposing in the Middle Ages to regulate sexual and family norms had the effect of disrupting the fundamental social institution of extended families and clans which had prevailed across Europe—as anywhere else on Earth—for millennia until then, and which still constitutes the norm in the majority of contemporary human societies today (Henrich 2020; Schulz et al. 2019).

One of the main effects produced by these family policies—which involved formal prohibitions and sanctions, moral duties and taboos—was an unprecedented *relational mobility* in European regions more exposed to the influence of the Western Church. These bans forced people to establish new significant relationships beyond their families and close-knit communities, contributing to the emergence of new social institutions and voluntary associations, such as universities and markets. The analyses conducted by Schulz and colleagues show that longer exposure of populations to the Catholic Church predicts (i) a greater dismantlement of intensive kinship bonds and (ii) WEIRD psychological variations, such as increased impersonal prosociality, individualism, decisional autonomy, and lower propensity to conformism and deference to authority (Henrich 2020; Schulz et al. 2019).[7] Recent evidence also shows that weaker kin-

---

7   For reasons of synthesis, I deliberately choose not to consider *religiosity* as another important driver of prosociality: see in this respect Norenzayan

networks positively correlate with more participatory and democratic institutions (Schulz 2022).[8]

Market integration. A second important body of empirical data collected by Henrich and collaborators starting from the early 2000s reveals a significant correlation between experiences with (or even mere exposure to) market institutions and the development of higher levels of impersonal prosociality and inclusiveness (Henrich 2000; Henrich et al. 2004). Henrich and colleagues' groundbreaking cross-cultural studies in behavioral economics report that different cultural and institutional contexts significantly shape people's prosociality and other morally relevant cognitive and behavioral traits (e.g., trust, altruistic behavior, conceptions of fairness). In cross-cultural experiments involving the Ultimatum Game[9], people from WEIRD societies are more generous, and more likely to accept egalitarian offers compared to people living in social realities organized

---

et al. (2016), Shariff & Norenzayan (2007; 2011).

8   A further relevant body of evidence that, for reasons of space, I will not discuss here, concerns the influence of *residential mobility* on psychological and value change. As research in this field shows, greater residential mobility enhances people's trust in strangers and preference toward egalitarian norms, makes people more tolerant and less exclusivist, encourages individuals to create larger social networks, to be more open to novelty and new experiences, and even to engage in more creative thinking (Lun et al. 2012; Choi & Oishi 2020).

9   In the Utimatum Game (UG), one player (proposer) is given a certain amount of money and has to propose how to divide it between themselves and another player (respondent). The respondent can either accept or reject the offer: if the respondent accepts, the amount is distributed as proposed; if the respondent rejects, both players receive nothing. The UG has been a highly influential paradigm in experimental economics, and field experiments using it suggested significant insights for the descriptive study of morality. Above all, these and other experimental paradigms in behavioral economics (e.g., the Dictator Game, Public Goods Game, and Trust Game) can offer valuable information about peoples' sense of (un)fairness, in this case specifically revealing their willingness to punish offers they consider unfair (i.e., deviations from norms of fairness). As shown by seminal cross-cultural studies by Henrich and colleagues, people's sense of fairness and their willingness to punish offers perceived as unfair vary, sometimes radically, between societies and cultures.

around kin-based institutions, such as hunter-gatherers, herders, and subsistence farmers from over 20 different societies worldwide. The less integrated into markets societies are, the more the economic and altruistic behavior of the agents reflects the standards of rationality predicted by neoclassical economic models (i.e., maximizing individual utility). In contrast, people from WEIRD and other market-integrated societies systematically deviate from these standards (Ensminger & Henrich 2014). In the absence of institutions to regulate large-scale cooperative enterprises and challenges, people from less market-integrated societies are psychologically more egoistic (see also Knafo et al. 2009; Marlowe et al. 2008).

It is important to note, nonetheless, that these data do not show that higher levels of market exposure or integration merely produce self-interested and instrumental incentives for increased impersonal prosociality, such as "If I am honest and generous, I will sell more". While conditional incentives certainly play a role empirical evidence suggests that higher levels of impersonal prosociality typically prescribed by market norms (such as being fair and honest with anonymous subjects), can become so internalized that people also exhibit them even in anonymous, one-shot games—i.e., with people they they are unlikely to ever meet again and who would have little to no opportunity to punish them in the future, even indirectly (Rand et al. 2014). Furthermore, experimental evidence shows that higher levels of impersonal prosociality correlate with a greater propensity to engage in voluntary cooperative associations, and with the establishment of long-lasting and effective formal institutions (Rustagi et al. 2010). This suggests that differences in psychological traits can also explain differences in social institutions, and not only the other way around (more on this below).

Of course, these data do not imply that mere proximity to market institutions predicts unconditional or purely disinterested moral motivation. However, what matters here is the relevance of this evidence for evaluating the (im)plausibility of the hard-wiring thesis. Contrary to 'institutional bypassing' views (see Sauer 2019 and chapter 2 above), experimental evidence shows that market institutions do not simply *bypass* human psychology and produce positive outcomes as side effects, but they can also significantly *modify* human cognitive and behavioral traits, expanding the circle of human cooperation, inclusiveness, and moral concern (Buchanan 2020; Henrich 2020, chapters 6 and 9).

This conclusion could sound problematic, and a few additional considerations may be needed. It is not uncommon to encounter both in folk morality and academic reflection (within and outside WEIRD societies) negative moral evaluations of individualist, competitive, and calculative traits, which are often seen as emblematic of contemporary WEIRD societies. These and other WEIRD psychological traits[10] can certainly be problematized from a moral point of view (though this is not my main concern here). It should be noted, however, that even though, e.g., self-interest and competition are highly valued in WEIRD societies, empirical evidence shows that people from more market-integrated and industrialized contexts also display higher preferences for zero-sum gains in competitive scenarios when they are obtained by respecting norms of honesty, transparency and fairness, and devalue them when they are facilitated by partiality or favoritism (Henrich 2020, 294).[11] While this may sound paradoxical, individualism and altruism

---

10   As well as, of course, market institutions and economies. Deirdre McCloskey observes that "Richer and more urban people, contrary to what the magazines of opinion sometimes suggest, are less materialistic, less violent, less superficial than poor and rural people. Because people in capitalist countries already possess the material, they are less attached to their possessions than people in poor countries. And because they have more to lose from a society of violence, they resist it" (2010, 26). While this may be true, markets and capitalism do not exclusively have 'positive' effects on the psychology, motivations, and behavior of people in societies in which they are more present, since these systems often also create and reinforce oppressive hierarchies and inequalities in terms of wealth, health, and power, moral consideration and respect (see e.g., Buchanan 2020, 150-151; Kumar & Campbell 2022, 169; Gowdy 1999).

11   In this respect, it is worth noting that advocates of the hard-wiring view like Persson and Savulescu (2017, 290) identify *nepotism* as a ky example of a hard-wired psychological trait—a claim that is challenged by this and other empirical evidence showing significant cross-cultural variations in preferences for impartial procedures and norms of fairness.

are not, in fact, conflicting psychological traits.[12] On the contrary, empirical findings show that higher scores on individualism scales positively correlate with greater impersonal prosociality and non-reciprocal forms of altruism (ibid.; Rhoads et al. 2021).[13]

It is also important not to misunderstand this evidence as implying that affluence predicts WEIRD traits, such as greater impersonal prosociality, emancipative values, analytic thinking, and so forth. As Henrich notes, historical data clearly suggest that increased levels of income and material security have likely been a consequence, rather than a cause, of the radical psychological and cultural variations and mobility that followed the disruption of intensive kin-based institutions in Medieval Europe. Moreover, evidence indicates that shifts toward WEIRD traits occurred consistently among both wealthy and poor populations, suggesting that affluence alone plays no relevant role in shaping these psychological traits (Henrich 2020, 478-480).

---

12 Individualism should not be confused with self-interest or egoism. Technically, in the psychological, sociological and anthropological literature, individualistic values emphasize the importance of individual autonomy, projects and self-expression over conformity, the protection of one's community and tradition, and the respect for duties, roles and identities rigidly defined by them (Henrich 2020; Hofstede 2003; Triandis 1995; Welzel 2013, chapter 6).

13 I must emphasize, once again, that this evidence should not be understood as something like a 'praise for the West', nor as a defense of the idea that Western cultures or countries are inherently more 'moral' than others. What I have been reporting are sets of correlations between socio-cultural ecological variables and psychological constructs; there is no philosophy of history, destiny, nor claim of Western superiority here. As Sauer rightly observes, these "are not Western values any more than mathematics is, in any interesting sense, Arabic simply because that's where the numbers people do it in originated [...]. Certain scientific discoveries were, as it happens, first made in certain places rather than others. But these scientific discoveries are part of the universal heritage of humanity. They had to emerge somewhere, but they belong to everyone" (Sauer 2023, 87; see also Welzel 2013, 41-42). Incidentally, empirical research shows that Western values and traditions alone do not predict increases in emancipative values or impersonal prosociality (see Welzel 2013).

Existential security. In his latest work on cultural evolution—drawing on over fifty years of longitudinal and cross-cultural sociological research on value change from more than one hundred countries—Ronald Inglehart (2018) concluded that the massive psychological, behavioral and value shifts observed across various societies can be primarily explained by a progressive increase in levels of existential security in recent history. According to Inglehart, traits such as intensive kinship, strong in-group solidarity, distrust and hostility towards out-groups, moral, religious and political intolerance, and support for authoritarianism are all responses to the precariousness of survival (see also Jost et al. 2003; Tropp 2012, 116). When basic resources are scarce, the risk that there might be just enough either for my tribe or yours can be high. But prosperity amplifies opportunities of interaction and cooperation, favoring both psychological and institutional change. In the 20th century, many societies in the post-war era began to experience unprecedented levels of wealth and peace. Probably for the first time in history, several generations in WEIRD countries grew up taking their survival for granted. According to Inglehart, this increase in existential security led to the emergence of radically new values, beliefs, and motivations, which in turn contributed to the rise of emancipatory social movements and more inclusive, fair, and democratic institutions (see also Buchanan 2020, chapter 5).

These radical changes in recent history encompass global trends such as the abolition of slavery; the emancipation of women, LGBTQ+ people, migrants, children, and disabled individuals; the reduction of several forms of discrimination and oppression (based on ethnic, religious, political or gender identities); the partial abolition of extreme forms of punishment (such as the death penalty); the institution of international norms against military aggressions, neo-colonialism and apartheid; increasing concern for the condition of non-human animals, ecosystems, and future generations.

Modern moralities are far more inclusivist, farsighted, and less biased than what we would expect if the hard-wiring thesis were true. There are several reasons, supported by evidence, for claiming so. First, many people (especially in WEIRD societies) nowadays believe that moral principles should apply universally (Henrich

2020). More and more people reject the idea that something can be morally acceptable for one group (such as men) but not for another (such as women), without a good reason for claiming so. Features like ethnicity, gender, or religion are considered irrelevant when determining who deserves basic moral rights and protections. This shift towards equality is evident in legal frameworks established to fight discrimination based on race, ethnicity, or gender, and the resources devoted to enforcing these laws are significant. Global attitudes toward racial and ethnic minorities have seen significant changes, particularly in the last decade.

Social movements such as *Black Lives Matter* have played a crucial role in raising awareness about racial injustice, sysyemic discrimination, and institutionalized violence toward black people Similar protests and changes have occurred in several countries, indicating a global shift in perception and action regarding racial justice. Empathy for refugees and migrants has increased despite ongoing political opposition in many world regions. Humanitarian organizations like the UNHCR have reported that public support for refugees has grown over the past decade. For example, a 2024 study reported that 73 percent of 33,197 adults from 52 countries believe refugees should be welcomed into their country (although there has been a slight decline compared to 2022 following the Russian invasion of Ukraine) (Ipsos & UNHCR 2024).

Public attitudes toward the growing migratory crisis have seen a moral shift, with many people acknowledging the duty to provide asylum and humanitarian aid to people fleeing war, persecution, or climate-related disasters.

Over the past century, feminist movements have fought against several issues such as political and economic discrimination, systemic violence and harassment. While patriarchal systems still subordinate women, significant progress have been made in many areas over the decades, albeit predominantly benefiting white women. Domestic labor and childcare responsibilities, though still unequal, are more balanced than they were in the past; women now have access to education, occupations, and positions of power previously dominated by men. Despite ongoing challenges, women in many parts of the world enjoy higher status, greater freedom, and increased respect compared to the past. Movements such as *#MeToo* have brought global attention to issues of sexual harassment, assault, and gender discrimination. The movement has not only led to widespread cultural change but has also inspired legal reforms to fight discrimination and violence against women (World Bank 2024). Support for gender equality in education, the workforce, and leadership roles has also increased. Nonetheless, more recently approximately half of interviewees across 31 countries (51%) believe that men are being asked to take on too much responsibility in supporting gender equality. Similarly, nearly half (46%) feel that efforts to promote women's equality have gone so far that they now discriminate against men. Also, Gen Z and Millennials are more likely than older generations to view a man who stays at home to care for his children as "less of a man" and to feel that the push for equal rights for women has already gone far enough (Ipsos 2024).

Modern political activists frequently highlight the persistency of racism and sexism in our society. While these phenomena remain, history reveals not only how entrenched they once were, but also the significant change that many societies have undergone over the past few decades. In the past, discriminatory practices were not only institutionalized but also normalized and widely accepted and tolerated (as violence was as well, more so than today: see Pinker 2011). Attitudes toward race and gender have now transformed drastically. Advocating for racist or sexist behavior or laws today—especially in WEIRD societies—are immediately met with stronger and more widespread condemnation.

Sexual morality is also changing. Societies across the world have displayed a wide range of sexual moralities. In ancient Greece, for example, homosexual relationships between older and younger men were welcomed. But for most of human history, gay people have been met with severe social stigma, discrimination, and hostility. Sexual norms are often treated as objective and irrefutable, in the same way that racist attitudes once labeled interracial relationships as repugnant. In numerous countries, same-sex relationships are not only criminalized but are also condemned by societal standards and bolstered by religious ideologies that dehumanize gay individuals (and other deviations from heteronormativity).

Nevertheless, in the past decades, significant improvements have been made for gay people (again, especially in WEIRD societies). People's attitudes have undergone a profound transformation (Aksoy et al. 2020; Haerpfer et al. 2022). Public attitudes toward gay people have softened and offensive language is less frequently used. Being openly gay no longer leads to the public shame or ostracism it once did.

Climate activism is another arena where concern for distant vulnerable subjects has surged. Climate change disproportionately affects low-income communities and future generations. Social movements such as Fridays for Future, Extinction Rebellion and others have galvanized millions, particularly young people, to advocate for policies that protect vulnerable populations from the worst impacts of climate disasters. More and more people view climate change as a pressing moral issue that requires immediate action (Hickman et al. 2021). The Paris Agreement (2015) and subsequent international efforts reflect a growing global recognition that climate change is not only an environmental issue but also a moral one, with concerns about the impacts on the world's poorest regions and future generations. Especially in WEIRD societies, public opinion has shifted to support stronger climate regulations and actions aimed at protecting those who are most vulnerable to its effects.

Another, less 'recent' but even more universal(ist) phenomenon is the global rise of human rights norms, which assert that all individuals should be treated as equals regardless of the local legal system or the specific advantages individuals may provide. In recent years, there has been a decline in the respect for many human rights around the world, largely due to wars. Although individuals often perceive themselves as having little impact on influencing geopolitical dynamics, this does not mean there hasn't been a shift in people's psychology and values. Consider, for example, the number of individuals in WEIRD societies who oppose Israel's actions against the Palestinian population, as well as the social mobilizations worldwide in support of Palestinians.

Additionally, people have increasingly acknowledged the moral rights of individuals who do not provide direct benefits to society

(Buchanan & Powell 2018). It is now widely believed that even when it would be possible to exploit or oppress a vulnerable minority without harming the larger group, doing so is morally wrong. Similarly, people who lack certain abilities—such as young children or severely disabled individuals—are seen as deserving of access to social resources and are not excluded from moral consideration.

Moreover, although the number of animals treated inhumanely and killed every day has in fact increased dramatically over the centuries and decades, the moral consideration of non-human animals has been rising in recent decades (Singer 2023). There is a widespread consensus that mistreatment of animals is wrong not just because of human interests, but because animals themselves have moral value. These beliefs have led to laws increasing regulation of farming conditions, minimizing animal suffering, and imposing strict regulations on the use of animals in research, and banning cruel practices like blood sports. Surveys and public opinion polls show rising support for ethical treatment of animals and greater awareness of factory farming practices. These growing concerns are reflected in the rise of plant-based diets and veganism, which have increased over the past few years (Mathieu & Richie 2022).

Another piece of evidence showing the ability to care about faraway strangers in need is the increasingly widespread voluntary action taken by individuals and organizations aimed at helping the world's most disadvantaged people (Charities Aid Foundation 2024). Even in times of global economic crisis, people increasingly engage in acts of kindness toward strangers. Unlike government-to-government aid, which may be motivated by national interests, private charitable giving is often driven by genuine, non-instrumental concern.

Let us now return to Inglehart's theory. Shifts in recent history concerning all these issues have been assessed by longitudinal and cross-cultural empirical research both with objective (O) and subjective measures (S), e.g., increasing women employment in positions of high social relevance (O) and people's attitudes towards this trend (S); national laws allowing same-sex marriage (O) and individual perceptions/attitudes towards it (S); and so forth. Inglehart understands these recent global trends of cultural change in terms of a shift from 'Materialist' to 'Post-Materialist' values (see Inglehart 2018, chapter 2).

Following Inglehart's theory, for instance, the growing acceptance of gender equality and homosexuality in contemporary societies can be explained by increasing levels of existential security. In agrarian societies, high fertility rates are encouraged because they provide an important means of subsistence in lack of efficient social security systems. According to Inglehart, this leads to developing norms that oppress women and stigmatize sexual behaviors not aimed at reproduction (see also Buchanan 2020, 124-125: surplus reproductive success leads to the 'Great Uncoupling', i.e., moralities become untethered from the demands of reproductive fitness; see also Kumar & Campbell 2022 for alternative, although compatible, explanations).

Inglehart's theory is robust and valuable because it allows to explain value change in all directions: not only inclusivist and/or emancipatory shifts, but also contractions of the circle of cooperation, moral consideration and respect. His research shows that exclusivist contractions of these circles are often caused by environmental or socio-economic crises, which hamper impersonal prosociality and emancipative values, foster stronger in-group favoritism, out-group stigmatization and dehumanization, exacerbate structural inequalities and power dynamics, and facilitate the rise of authoritarianism, which in turn reduces people's freedom.

Inglehart's conclusions overlap with Buchanan's (2020), and Buchanan and Powell's (2018) theories of moral change on several points. What emerges from both accounts is an extremely plastic and flexible view of human morality and moral psychology, since empirical evidence shows that human cognition, motivation and behavior can be either exclusivist and hostile or inclusivist and cooperative depending on the circumstances. Tribalistic, shortsighted and hostile responses are more likely to activate when cues associated with existential threats—such as competition for scarce resources or the risk of contracting diseases—are detected (Buchanan & Powell 2018, 189). However, in the absence or reduction of these conditions, tribalistic attitudes diminish, making it easier to implement more prosocial and farsighted capacities and behaviors, as well as openness to new ideas and possibilities (ibid.; Inglehart 2018).[14]

This view portrays a picture of the human mind that also coheres with evolutionary neurobiological models emphasizing brain plasticity. According to these views, information-processing brain structures are significantly shaped by the environment, and not the predetermined, fixed result of genetic specification. Against the massive modularity hypothesis, neurobiological evidence on brain plasticity suggests that evolution has not definitively selected and designed specific brain modules rigidly adapted to the ancestral environments of the Pleistocene, but rather selected a brain that is still wide open to change and able to adapt to its environment (Buller 2005, 134-136; Kumar & Campbell 2022; Sterelny 2010).[15] Powell & Buchanan (2016, 246) compared this environment-dependent plasticity of the human mind to the sophisticated armor that certain water fleas develop only if they detect chemical elements indicating the presence of predators or other existential threats (for further evidence on adaptive phenotypic plasticity, see Stoks et al. 2016; Reger et al. 2018; Watkins 2021). As recent empirical research and cultural evolutionary models suggest, the influence of culture on human psychology, behavior (and phenotype more generally) is

---

14   Although scholars like Inglehart have shown that increased levels of existential security correlate with variations in several psychological traits (e.g., trust, self-control), nobody has proved yet that better material conditions *alone* predict psychological shifts in typically WEIRD cognitive and perceptual abilities (such as analytic thinking, the emphasis on intentionality in moral judgment, the experience of guilt over shame, etc.). On the contrary, the main factors highlighted by Henrich—e.g., variations in family institutions, market integration/exposure, etc.— *predict* several WEIRD psychological variations, highlighting more clearly the causal links between variables.

15   I want to stress, once again, that this is one of the most relevant elements of disagreement between my account and Buchanan's (2020). According to Buchanan, moralities *but not moral psychology* (or 'the moral mind') are flexible and not rigidly fixed by evolution. My view is more radical, as I argue that that empirical evidence provides reasons to believe that not only moralities but also moral psychology is far more flexible than many have recently claimed. I am grateful to Allen Buchanan for prompting me to highlight this point.

so profound that it can even significantly shape human physiology and anatomical structures (Henrich 2015; 2020; Sterelny 2012; Wrangham 2009). This evidence paints a picture of human moral psychology and behavior as the extremely plastic and malleable result of several flexible cultural, societal, and cognitive mechanisms, rather than being rigidly constrained by adaptations to the ancestral conditions of EEA, embedded in our genes and hard-wired into human brains.

4.3. *Limits and critical considerations*

The evidence reported in the previous sections challenges the hard-wiring thesis and its evolutionary explanations. On the one hand, the idea that tribalistic, biased, and exclusivist traits have been selected in the Pleistocene and still strongly influence human behavior contrasts with evidence and theoretical advancements in psychological, sociological and anthropological research. On the other hand, recent longitudinal and cross-cultural studies report that profound psychological and value variations can occur even in relatively short time-spans, portraying human cognition, values, and morality as highly plastic and malleable (see, for instance, Lun et al. 2012; Choi & Oishi 2020).

Nonetheless, this evidence also depicts psychological and moral change as highly dependent on macro-level socio-environmental conditions, whose dynamics are often difficult and costly for individuals to understand and control. Buchanan and Powell's naturalistic theory of moral change (2016; 2018)[16] emblematically

---

16　Buchanan and Powell developed a comprehensive theory of moral *progress*. However, as stated above, I am mostly interested in their underlying descriptive-explanatory theory of moral change. I will thus focus on this latter by looking at the moral shifts they deem progressive from an empirical, naturalized perspective, i.e., setting aside normative and metaethical considerations about why such changes should be deemed good or desirable (on this point, see Bina 2024). In other words, I will mostly focus on why and how some of the moral shifts they have in mind occurred or may occur, i.e., on their enabling conditions.

represents this view: in their account, inclusivist and emancipatory shifts occur only under favorable socio-ecological conditions. As they put it, moral inclusiveness and emancipative values are 'luxury goods' (2018, 210–17; see also Buchanan 2020).

I am sympathetic with most of Buchanan and Powell's view. Among contemporary accounts of moral change, their account is one of the few acknowledging the scientific plausibility of significant moral and cognitive plasticity and flexibility.[17] However, their theory appears unable to provide a sufficiently convincing *naturalistic* account of the enabling conditions for the increase and exercise of a specific type of psychological-moral shift, that is, increases in agency (see Bina 2024b), or what they call 'open-ended' normativity, as and its causal role in promoting macro-level moral change. The critical considerations I will now raise against Buchanan and Powell also apply to other accounts of moral change that are more explicitly materialist, supra-individualist, and/or structuralist-institutionalist in nature (e.g., Sauer 2023). These accounts, in fact, are even less capable of explaining how changes in psychological capacities, particularly increases in agency, can drive further psychological shifts, as well as contribute to cultural evolution and institutional transformation. As mentioned above, for some of these views this is not even much of an issue: they are eliminativist about these factors, believing that significant moral change can be explainable without reference to them (Sauer 2019; 2023).

Above all, Buchanan and Powell's view faces a methodological-explanatory dilemma:

(i) First, they could acknowledge endorsing a materialist, structuralist-institutionalist view, attributing strong causal priority to factors and dynamics largely beyond agential control, significantly downplaying the causal role of agency in the explanation of the instances of moral change they primarily address. However, by doing so, they expose their theory to critiques of environmental or

---

17 For another view significantly concerned with moral-cognitive plasticity and the psychological dimension of moral change, see Kumar & Campbell (2022).

socio-structural determinism. Buchanan and Powell are ambiguous on this point: they explicitly state not to endorse such a view, but their theory often seems to point in that direction.

(ii) Alternatively, if they claim to attribute a significant *causal* role to factors such as human agency, open-ended moral reasoning and normativity in the dynamics of moral change, their theory appears unable to fully account for the enabling conditions and causal impact of these factors on broader societal shifts in fully naturalistic terms. Buchanan & Powell provide neither a theory nor evidence to suggest how these capacities can emerge and develop; how their exercise and improvement could be facilitated, or how these "moral powers" (2018, 50) they refer to play a causal role in the broader societal shifts they discuss.

A closer analysis of the two horns of this dilemma will show that neither option constitutes a satisfactory naturalistic account of moral change.

Buchanan (2020, 139-143) sought to address this shortcoming in two ways: first, by providing an evolutionary explanation of *moral consistency reasoning* (hereafter, MCR; see Campbell & Kumar 2012) based on a 'partner choice' hypothesis; second, by emphasizing the fundamental motivational role of moral identity in engaging in MCR. However, both MCR and moral identity are conceptually distinct from the notions of agency and open-ended normativity. First, in Buchanan's view, MCR has a clear evolutionary and social function—namely, being perceived as reliable and predictable cooperative partners—whereas agency and open-ended normativity do not necessarily fulfill that function. On the contrary, the defining feature of open-ended normativity is precisely its detachment from any clearly specified functional normativity (see Buchanan 2012). Moreover, agency includes motivation while MCR does not (see Bina 2024); and while agency and open-ended normativity are characterized by counterfactual and prospective thinking, MCR is primarily a systematization of existing beliefs and intuitions. Finally, MCR appears to be an overly demanding indicator of partner reliability (it is difficult to imagine social actors inferring the trustworthiness of their partner based on how well they engage in MCR—especially given that what counts as good MCR remains a matter of dispute even among professional scholars in the field). Second, Buchanan's conception of moral identity seems to concern the capacity to be more faithful to certain values and groups, but not the ability to engage in critical moral reasoning detached from biological and social norms. Again, it seems overly optimistic to assume that people are motivated to be perceived by others as agents who excel in sophisticated MCR. This may hold true for a small subset of individuals, but it is unlikely to be generalizable.

Horn (i). On the one hand, if a theory of moral change like Buchanan & Powell's emphasized a strong one-way causal dependence of micro-level psychological and value change on macro-level socio-environmental conditions—without including factors such as agency or conscious reasoning—it risks exposing itself to accusations of materialism or environmental/socio-structural determinism, i.e., the view according to which "ultimately, broadly 'material' forces are responsible for driving people's values or, at the very least, for providing the fertile ground that allows values whose time has come to thrive" (Sauer 2023, 87). While this perspective may not be inherently problematic, I am not convinced that Buchanan and Powell would fully endorse it. If we agree that supra-individual, socio-environmental conditions and dynamics are difficult to understand and control, and social structures to change, then depicting psychological and value change as so contingent on these factors risks presenting a view of human psychology, values, behavior, and moralities as largely immune to autonomous and consciously designed projects of reform.

One might counter that this concern arises only if Buchanan and Powell consider the socio-environmental enabling conditions they identify as not only necessary but also sufficient for moral change. However, Buchanan and Powell seem to suggest this interpretation in several passages, such as the flea's armor analogy. Other critics have noted that, according to Buchanan and Powell, "Socio-cultural innovations that alleviate infectious disease, resource scarcity, physical insecurity, interethnic conflict and low rates of productivity *suffice* to foster inclusive morality" (Persson & Savulescu 2017, 287; cf. Powell & Buchanan 2016, 247).

Moreover, by taking this position Buchanan and Powell appear to concede too much to pessimistic or conservative perspectives, suggesting that efforts aimed at inclusivist moral and social change are futile or unachievable in 'non-luxurious' contexts. If external conditions are not sufficiently favorable to enable inclusivist moral shifts, any effort toward reform would seem in vain—yet it is often precisely in harsh social conditions where these changes are most needed. Should people give up or passively wait for material or institutional conditions to improve?

Buchanan and Powell's theory would avoid collapsing into a purely materialist or structuralist-institutionalist account if it could explain not only what enables the exercise or improvements of human moral capacities—both in favorable and unfavorable conditions—but also whether and how the agential capacities they refer to can influence broader structural-institutional dimensions of morality. Can psychological change and the exercise of agential capacities contribute to structural-institutional moral change even under harsh socio-ecological conditions?

Horn (ii). Buchanan and Powell may reject the first horn of the dilemma, i.e., the critique accusing them of positing an overly strong dependence of moral change on environmental and material conditions. They could argue that their theory also aims to account for other factors in the dynamics of moral change, and that material, structural, and environmental conditions are not sufficient to explain significant moral shifts, including psychological ones. Indeed, parochial, conformist, exclusivist, intolerant, oppressive, authoritarian, and myopic psychological traits are widely present in human populations even under what Buchanan and Powell consider luxurious material and institutional conditions. What happens when favorable material conditions do not correlate with increased prosocial, inclusivist, egalitarian, and emancipative psychological and value shifts? Buchanan and Powell attempt to explain this phenomenon by suggesting that tribalism and exclusivist traits and institutions can emerge and stabilize even even in the absence of actual existential threats, as long as such threats are perceived as real, for example as the result of ideological or demagogic manipulation (Buchanan & Powell 2018, chapters 6-7)[18,19]

Although this hypothesis is plausible, its general explanatory power remains limited. While the socio-environmental circumstances discussed in the previous sections certainly play(ed) a significant role in shaping human psychology toward greater impersonal prosociality and the development of emancipative values and institutions, they still appear insufficient—and perhaps even *unnecessary*—to fully explain these changes. Even taking into account phenomena such as ideology and demagogic manipulation, we still lack a more accurate understanding of the micro-level mechanisms involved in moral change dynamics—both inclusivist and exclusivist, emancipative and oppressive. For example, why are certain individuals and groups more or less susceptible to such influences? Under what conditions,

---

18   Taking into account the *subjective* perception of one's existential condition—along with more 'objective' measures (e.g., well-being, institutional stability)—is highly relevant for understanding people's social and moral psychology. For instance, Rhoads and colleagues (2021) found strong correlations between levels of subjective well-being (self-reported life satisfaction), self-expression values, and various prosocial behaviors. These findings could be explained by the fact that several forms of impersonal prosociality, such as non-reciprocal (or non-conditional) forms of altruism, are often driven by autonomous decisions rather than being prescribed by the norms and expectations of one's close-knit community (more on this below).

19   Buchanan and Powell call 'moral regressions' those exclusivist shifts and conservative or reactionary pressures directed against expansions of the moral circle or their institutional stabilization (2018, chapter 7). At the beginning of this work, I stated my intention to address the phenomenon of moral change, as much as possible, in neutral, descriptive terms. I will therefore adhere to distinctions such as inclusivism vs. exclusivism, impersonal prosociality vs. intensive kinship (or tribalism), emancipatory vs. patriarchal values, and so on. These concepts are less controversial than the ideas of moral *progress* and *regress* from the naturalistic perspective adopted here, as their meaning does not depend on substantive normative or metaethical views, and (also for these reasons) they are likely more immediately intelligible to a wider audience.

and through what means, can these influences be avoided or countered (see Zmigrod et al. 2021; Zmigrod 2022)?

If Buchanan and Powell were to take the second route—i.e., to remain open to additional explanatory factors—without abandoning to their naturalistic methodology, their account of moral change would still appear methodologically and empirically incomplete, and not particularly useful from a practical standpoint. The enabling conditions they emphasize appear insufficient to retrospectively understand the dynamics underlying the type of psychological moral change that constitutes the common focus of our works. Even more importantly, their account appears inadequate for developing prospective empirically-informed and effective strategies to foster (or avoid) further changes—something their theory explicitly aims to provide (2018, 31): How can we steer material conditions, institutions, and social structures in the direction we deem most justified if not through reflection, social critique, and action, or by encouraging others to adopt alternative ways of reasoning and acting to promote common goals?

What, then, besides material conditions can lead people to change how they reason about morally relevant issues? What drives people to decide either instinctively and inflexibly (e.g., under the influence of natural inclinations, habits, or local socio-cultural norms) or, alternatively, through more careful consideration of options, information, interests, and reasons? I believe that failing to address this question constitutes one of the greatest weaknesses of contemporary accounts of moral change. In what follows, I aim to fill this gap.

5.

EXPLAINING OPEN-ENDED NORMATIVITY: MORALITY AS AN EXAPTATION

5.1. *Agency and open-ended normativity: evolutionary mysteries?*

So far, the main aim of this work has been to show that psychological moral change beyond tribalism, parochialism and shortsightedness has occurred extensively across societies, especially in recent history. Empirical evidence indicates that, under certain ecological circumstances, even people's *motivations*—and not only their beliefs (a major concern expressed, e.g., by Persson and Savulescu 2017)—have shifted towards greater levels of moral inclusivity, impersonal prosociality, farsightedness, and emancipation. Although there is no reason to believe that this process will necessarily continue, some of these changes are ongoing, and there seem to be no compelling reasons to believe that humanity (who?, where?) has reached a definitive and genetically specified limit to moral inclusiveness, emancipation, and cooperation[1]. The plausibility of the hard-wiring thesis appears significantly diminished.

Morality is a far more complex phenomenon than what has been outlined so far. The phenomenology of moral experience involves more than merely trusting or helping (or not) strangers, avoiding to discriminate against them, or refraining from being violent in competition for scarce resources. Some of these (and other) behaviors are now relatively well-specified and required by formal and informal

---

1   See Sauer (2019), Persson & Savulescu (2017). Although Sauer believes that human psychology is destined to remain tribalistic, he contentds that societal-institutional ('supra-individual') moral progress is likely to continue (Sauer 2023). A similar thesis is also present in Kumar & Campbell (2022), who, however, defend a more flexible view of human psychology.

norms and institutions—especially in WEIRD societies—whose foundations and justifications would likely be endorsed by most readers of this book. Some of these behaviors are even encouraged by effective systems of sanctions and incentives that—paired with other mechanisms—make them more easily internalizable, habitual, and widespread.

However, certain contemporary problems—including the very possibility of being critical towards received moral and non-moral principles, norms and judgements—are more controversial and complex than others. While no unequivocally correct answers can often be given to these issues, some moral problems require careful contextual examination, information-gathering, reasoning and justification. Morality does not merely require *feeling* or *behaving* in specific ways; it also involves the distinctive activity of critically reflecting, deliberating, and justifying choices, judgements, and norms concerning complex interpersonal and collective problems (see Songhorian et al. 2022).

Certain social practices, moral norms and principles may be (or may become over time) relatively uncontroversial in theory, although they can still remain difficult to implement in practice.[2] Others, however, are much more controversial in theory, which can also make their implementation more difficult. Cases of the former kind mainly concern motivation; cases of the latter kind concern reasoning.[3] The evidence discussed so far indicates that favorable socio-ecological circumstances largely predict changes in people's motivations, dispositions to trust, self-control, and other multi-purpose or domain-general capacities involved in moral experiences,

---

2   Several scholars have suggested that as the circle of moral consideration expands, it becomes increasingly difficult to practically satisfy the normative demands arising from this extension. See, e.g., Asma (2012), Goldsmith & Posner (2005), Haidt (2012), Persson & Savulescu (2017).

3   Such a theoretical distinction does not imply that reasoning and motivation should be kept separate: reasoning can, at least in part, contribute to determining moral judgement and action (see Sauer 2017; May 2013), and non-doxastic motivations are known to influence moral reasoning (Bago & De Neys 2019; Haidt 2001; Kunda 1990; Mercier & Sperber 2017).

reasoning, and decision-making. In what follows, we will see how and why moral agents can combine these capacities together in different ways that are relevant to the present discourse.[4]

As we saw in the previous sections, evolutionary psychologists face significant challenges in accounting for the selection of a costly cognitive capacity for engaging in sophisticated moral reasoning, as quicker and cheaper solutions such as emotions and heuristics are often more efficient for addressing moral problems. Nonetheless, some scholars have suggested that the emergence of such a capacity might be explained by its advantage in providing post-hoc rationalizations for controversial judgments or actions, making them more acceptable to others and thereby reducing the risks of violent reactions, punishments, or social exclusion (Haidt 2001; 2012; Mercier & Sperber 2017). According to this view, however, this capacity plays no *ex-ante* causal role in the determination of moral judgment and behavior, which are seen as direct results of emotionally charged reactions of approval and disapproval (Haidt 2001; 2012). Recently, several scholars have criticized this view (see Campbell & Kumar 2012; Fine 2006; Railton 2014; Sauer 2012; 2017; Songhorian et al. 2022, section 4).

---

4   While actual behavior and social outcomes should certainly be among the primary objects of analysis in a theory of moral change, in a series of works (Bina 2023; Bina 2024a, chapter 1; Bina 2024b; Songhorian et al. 2022), I have argued that such a theory (and a theory of morality more broadly) should also account for variations in the 'internal' cognitive processes involved in moral decisions, rather than focusing solely on observable behavior and its effects on the world. This thesis might be misunderstood as evaluative, but here I conceive it primarily as methodological. Regardless of which of these aspects matters more from a moral point of view, my position simply acknowledges that each level of analysis can be studied empirically, that all play a relevant causal role in shaping the social reality, and that we possess reliable knowledge and tools to intervene on each of these levels. Whether this methodological approach is viewed as an a-priori theoretical assumption or as an empirical observation, I believe that such a pluralistic methodology offers a more comprehensive model for understanding social reality, as well as greater opportunities to change it (especially once we understand the links and relationships between different levels of analysis. See Madva 2016).

The evidence and models discussed in the previous chapters do not account for the causal role played by moral reasoning in the dynamics of moral change. Moreover, with a few exceptions (Buchanan 2020; Campbell & Kumar 2012; Kumar & Campbell 2022; Huemer 2016; Singer 1981/2011; Songhorian 2022) many recent contributors to the debate on moral progress who adopt a naturalistic and broad historical and global perspective on moral change tend to reject (or significantly downplay) the causal role of moral reasoning in promoting inclusivist moral shifts and emancipative values (Hopster 2019; Rorty 1999; Severini 2021; Smyth 2020; Tam 2020).

As already emphasized, data and theories discussed in the previous chapters suggest a strong dependence of psychological and value change on environmental and socio-economic circumstances. Specifically, harsh conditions seem to correlate with hostility, discrimination, tribalism, myopia, exclusivism, deference to tradition and authority, while prosperity leads to greater cooperation, inclusivity, and open-mindedness. So conceived, these models leave little room for the possibility of active, intentional, and reasoned projects for moral reform. By depicting changes in moral beliefs, attitudes, and motivations as heaviliy dependent on external circumstances and supra-individual dynamics rather than on human agency, this view undermines the very idea of 'open-ended' moral normativity and its potential for change.[5]

---

5   An alternative approach may consider social, cultural and moral changes that appear too 'big' for our limited evolved psychologies as relying on a sort of external 'extension' or 'scaffolding' of human cognition (see, e.g., Gallagher 2013; Sauer 2019). To my knowledge, a systematic theory of the 'extended moral mind' has yet to be formulated. However, I suspect that, if developed, such a theory would still need to directly address the plausibility of the hard-wiring thesis. One must either believe that significant moral shifts (e.g., emancipatory, inclusivist) can only occur 'outside' individual minds, due to the evolved constraints of human psychology (Sauer 2019; 2023), or acknowledge that these kinds of moral change can both drive and result from substantial individual psychological change. My current research inclines me towards the latter view, which I see as less reductionist and more pluralistic on a methodological level. Henrich and colleagues' work is the strongest evidence in its support.

The concept of 'open-ended normativity' refers to the capacity to deviate from the strong external influence of various kinds of normativity to which human psychology, behavior, and moralities are often subjected.[6] Buchanan and Powell consider this capacity a necessary condition for the realization of inclusivist shifts, claiming that "any naturalistic explanation of inclusivist morality must feature the capacity for open-ended normativity" (2015, 65). Unfortunately, however, Buchanan and Powell fail to explain, even in minimally naturalistic terms, why and how this capacity emerged and could be developed, implemented, and improved. The authors limit themselves assuming its existence as a fact, providing only a few anecdotal examples and failing to explain what might favor or hinder it. As they themselves admit, "It is clear that this capacity exists [...] even if we do not possess a good account of the conditions under which the capacity is likely to be effectively exercised" (2015, 64).

Buchanan and Powell are not merely stating that we currently lack convincing explanations for the emergence and development of this capacity. Their claim is much more radical: they contend that the ability for open-ended normativity, like the inclusivist moral shifts that they argue necessarily depend on it, cannot be accounted for by *any* evolutionary explanation, "whether of the selectionist or by-product variety" (2015, 38)[7].

Above, I presented some skeptical considerations about the idea that a specific capacity for moral cognition could be considered an adaptation—i.e., that it was selected for and continues to perform a

---

6　For instance, according to several evolutionary models, many social norms in virtually every culture were selected because of their contribution to enhancing biological fitness (Haidt 2012; Joyce 2006; Tomasello 2016).

7　It is no coincidence that Buchanan and Powell refer to these shifts as "inclusivist anomalies". The main reasons behind this claim are that (a) adaptationist hypotheses explain the selection of traits by referring to specific biological functions, but the capacity for open-ended moral reasoning doesn't seem to have a clear one; and (b) by-product hypotheses are essentially just-so-stories (i.e., *ad hoc* conjectures lacking a solid scientific foundation). As I argued in the previous chapters, (a) is a plausible claim. However, as I will argue below, (b) is problematic.

clear fitness-enhancing function. However, as mentioned earlier, not every evolved trait is an adaptation. Some traits cannot be explained by referring to the function(s) they perform within a particular ecological system; nevertheless, their emergence and persistence can still be explained as the scientifically and logically plausible consequence of the selection of other traits, or the combination or co-optation of traits for uses that differ from the original function for which they were selected.

As introduced above, these derivative traits are known in the literature as evolutionary by-products, a specific subset of which are known as *exaptation*s (see Gould & Lewontin 1979; Gould & Vrba 1982; Buss et al. 1998). In their critiques of evolutionary explanations of morality, both Machery & Mallon (2010) and Buchanan & Powell (2015) not only rejected the idea that morality and moral cognition may be considered evolutionary adaptations, but also dismissed the possibility that they could be understood as by-products of other evolved traits (Buchanan & Powell 2015, 55-60; Machery & Mallon 2010, 23).

Although they presented several arguments and evidence against the idea that a specifically moral cognitive capacity technically 'evolved' (some of which I have reported above), Machery and Mallon provided no argument to substantiate their skepticism about conceiving moral cognition as a by-product of other evolved traits. On the contrary, they suggest that

> the capacity to grasp moral norms and the capacity to make moral judgments might be similar to chess or handwriting. The capacities to play chess and to write involve various evolved cognitive traits (e.g., visual recognition and memorization of rules for the former), but they did not evolve. Similarly, we conjecture that the capacity to grasp moral norms and the capacity to make moral judgments involve various evolved cognitive traits (including [...] a disposition to grasp norms in general), but they themselves did not evolve (Machery & Mallon 2010, 23).

In other words, their view is that moral cognition arises as a consequence of other evolved traits, such as basic building blocks of social cognition in animals (e.g., emotions) or a distinctive capacity for normative cognition. However, this closely resembles what a by-products explanation of moral cognition would entail. We might agree with Machery and Mallon that moral cognition was not *directly* selected in functionalist-adaptationist terms (i.e., because of its direct contribution to improving reproductive fitness), but to deny that its emergence as a by-product of other capacities constitutes a plausible evolutionary explanation seems conceptually mistaken. To be fair, even Machery and Mallon's direct critique of adaptationist models of the evolution of morality (2010, 24-30) is not particularly compelling. Their argument proceeds as follows: models like reciprocal altruism and indirect reciprocity aim to explain the emergence of morality in adaptationist terms. While these models provide plausible explanations for the evolution of certain (limited) forms of reciprocity, prosociality, and cooperation, these mechanisms represent only a small part of morality. They conclude that morality is not an adaptation because these adaptationist models fail to account for the more impersonal and non-reciprocal aspects of morality. However, this conclusion does not imply that these latter forms of prosociality cannot be given *any* evolutionary explanation. It simply suggests that the explanatory scope of these specific adaptationist models is limited.

Buchanan and Powell (2015) offered slightly more developed but still inconclusive arguments against by-product explanations of moral cognition, particularly regarding the capacity for open-ended moral normativity. Their critique emphasizes that no current by-product explanation is sufficiently rigorous or detailed to conclude that open-ended moral reasoning and normativity are necessary implications of the selection of other traits—e.g., as the spotted hyena's hypertrophic clitoris is a necessary biological implication of its evolved increased aggressiveness (as a consequence of increased levels of testosterone), or as the Spandrels of San Marco (the triangular architectonic elements between the arches) are secondary but inevitable consequence of the design and construction of more fundamental structural elements (Buchanan & Powell 2015, 56; Gould & Lewontin 1979).

Some considerations are necessary regarding what can be technically considered a by-product, especially in relation to the degree of probability (or absolute necessity) by which an evolutionary 'spandrel' is supposed to follow from the selection of other traits. If by-products are defined only as *necessary* consequences of other traits, then we likely lack sufficient data and tools to conclude that the psychological traits enabling open-ended normativity are *necessary* consequences of the selection of other traits (e.g., emotions, empathy, theory of mind, domain-general reasoning abilities, or norm cognition). However, if this is the case, we also cannot assert, as both Machery & Mallon and Buchanan & Powell do, that they are certainly *not* by-products. The possibility that the cognitive capacities enabling the development and exercise of open-ended moral reasoning and normativity are necessary consequences of the selection of other traits remains, in principle, absolutely plausible; that said, this does not imply that their implementation, or specific outcomes such as particular emancipatory or inclusivist shifts, are also necessary consequences of the selection of those traits.

If, on the other hand—as Buchanan and Powell actually seem to suggest—we can consider by-products *scientifically and logically plausible* (though not 100% certain) consequences of the selection of other traits, then asserting that open-ended morality and moral cognition can be understood as by-products becomes even less problematic. Moreover, as discussed in the previous sections, psychological traits can vary even rapidly under cultural pressures. The quantity and variety of potential influencing factors, combined with the speed of cultural evolution, render potential by-products explanations of cognitive traits such as open-ended moral reasoning qualitatively different from cases like San Marco or the spotted hyena's clitoris. We cannot reasonably demand the former adhere to the same minimalist and linear causal sequence required to explain the latter.

Although Buchanan and Powell "do not mean to advocate any mysterious or transcendental view" (2015, 65), their rejection of *any possible* evolutionary explanation for moral cognition, open-ended normativity, and inclusivist shifts render their view scientifically suspect, metaphysically problematic, and the characterization of their theory of moral change as 'naturalistic' conceptually incorrect (FitzPatrick 2019). Positing such a gap between scientifically grounded evolutionary principles and a distinctive ethical capacity and/or process that (i) operates independently of (or even radically against) these principles, and (ii) is unexplainable in scientifically or naturalistically plausible terms, evokes problematic dualisms in the history of evolutionary theory (Huxley 1893)[8]. Such a stance casts doubt on the very naturalistic methodology Buchanan and Powell claim to rely on in their work (2018, 26-30), bringing their theory closer to non-naturalistic accounts of morality and ethics (FitzPatrick 2019).[9] The limitations of these accounts undermine the very project of explaining open-ended moral cognition and robust inclusivist-emancipatory psychological moral shifts in fully naturalistic terms, and hence any ambition to use available scientific knowledge to design empirically-informed strategies for promoting moral reform (or avoiding undesirable shifts).

> Presumably, however, this capacity has been around for quite some time. Why, then, did the dynamic of expansive morality not happen earlier, or indeed later? Why did it happen, when it happened? This is, again, not problem that afflicts their [Buchanan & Powell's] theory specifically; rather, it is a formidable puzzle any theory of moral progress (or regress) must contend with (Sauer 2023, 53).

In the next section, I address this gap by exploring the possibility of explaining humans' capacities for open-ended moral reasoning and normativity as evolutionary by-products.

5.2. Enabling conditions for open-ended normativity: a naturalistic, cultural-evolutionary explanation of increases in agency and agency-driven moral change

---

8   Notably, a similar paradox was identified in Huxley's idea of a fundamental opposition between the natural-cosmic and the ethical process. Huxley's view in *Evolution and Ethics* is encapsulated in his famous metaphor depicting the cultural-ethical process as a gardener controlling the spontaneous processes of life and death in vegetation, which are naturally characterized by competition for resources and domination (on this point, see also Singer 2011, 62).

9   See Nagel (2012) for a somewhat isolated defense of the thesis that the apparent incompatibility between 'Darwinian' naturalism and our phenomenological experience and understanding of morality, freedom, and consciousness raises doubts about the former.

In what follows, I argue for a more optimistic view about the possibility of explaining agency-based moral change in naturalistic terms.[10] I propose a model that integrates the theories discussed above by emphasizing and clarifying the links between the macro (ecological, structural) and micro (psychological) levels of moral change. I outline a causal sequential model that explains (a) the cultural selection of psychological traits that enable (or hinder) agency and open-ended normativity, and (b) the role these traits play in the dynamics that lead to (or obstruct) macro-level structural-institutional shifts.[11]

My model rejects views that equate moral change solely with structural-institutional change, or that treat psychological change as merely an epiphenomenon of largely ungovernable supra-individual dynamics. On the contrary, my model posits that psychological moral change—i.e., changes in individuals agency, beliefs, reasoning abilities, attitudes, motivations, and other cognitive-behavioral traits and skills—can be both a product and a driver of broader structural-institutional shifts.[12]

To simplify, the general dynamics of moral change and the potential interactions between macro and micro levels can be illustrated using Coleman's 'bath-tub' model of social change (Coleman 1990, Fig. 1). According to this model, changes in macro-level socio-environmental conditions foster changes at the micro level of individual motivations, psychology, decision strategies, and action, which in turn contribute to further changes at the macro level of social structures and institutions.

---

10   By 'agency-based,' I refer to the idea that increased levels of agency can serve as the source, the objective, and the outcome of moral change (for further discussion, see Bina 2024b).

11   The basic structure of my model draws on a human development sequence proposed by Welzel and Inglehart (2010), but it substantially differs from it in (a) its specific focus on psychological change, agency, and open-ended normativity and (b) its reliance on a more pluralistic and empirically-grounded set of theoretical assumptions concerning human motivation.

12   According to Inglehart and Welzel, institutional change is often *preceded* and *caused* by psychological and value change, rather than the other way around (Inglehart 2018, 3; Welzel 2007; 2013, 38; Welzel & Inglehart 2010).

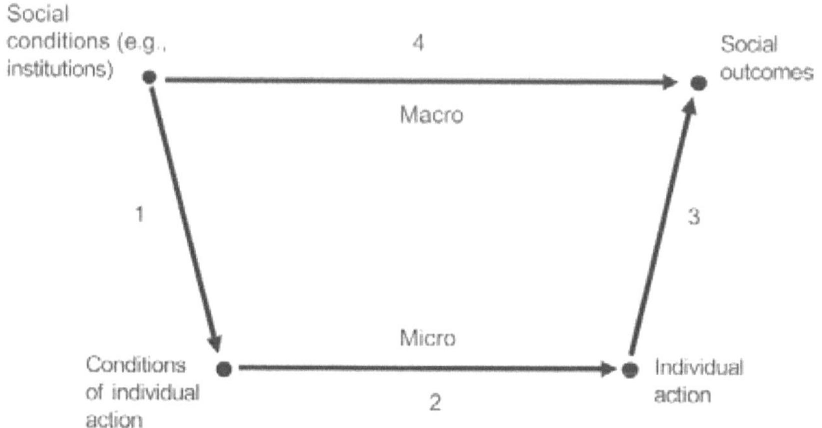

Fig. 1. *The bath-tub model of social change.*

In previous sections, I reported preliminary (and admittedly partial) evidence supporting links 1 and 2 of this process—i.e., psychological and value shifts fostered by environmental, structural, cultural, and/or institutional change. But what about links 2 and 3 and the node between them, which represents individual action? Can psychological and value changes enable (or hinder) the micro-level conditions necessary for greater agency and open-ended moral reasoning, and simultaneously drive macro-level social and moral change? If so, how?

Before addressing these questions, let us briefly summarize a few relevant theoretical points discussed so far. At the beginning of this work, I introduced an influential view in the contemporary debate on moral change: the idea that selective pressures in the Pleistocene favored a tribalistic, myopic, exclusivist psychology that is largely resistant to change and to 'ordinary' projects of moral reform. Proponents of this view argue that the timescales of biological evolution are extremely slow, and psychological evolution operates in a similar manner.

I then outlined some implications of accepting this view by examining two accounts of moral change proposed in recent years that rely on the hard-wiring thesis. One account emphasizes that significant psychological change beyond parochialism and myopia, as well as improvements in agency (i.e., enhanced reasoning *and* motivation) is impossible to achieve with ordinary socio-cultural means. Instead, proponents advocate for alternative, more effective strategies such as moral bioenhancement (Persson & Savulescu 2012; 2017). The other account asserts that psychological change plays no role in promoting significant moral shifts, which occur outside individual minds at the macro-level of social structures and institutions, and may even be facilitated by limited prosocial dispositions, self-interest, and desire for power, provided these traits are appropriately channeled through institutional mechanisms (Sauer 2019).

In chapters 3 and 4, I presented several considerations and lines of evidence showing that the empirical claims underlying these views are relatively weak. In particular, I highlighted that substantial psychological changes toward greater prosociality, normative emancipation, decisional autonomy, farsightedness, self-control (and more) have occurred throughout human evolution, especially in recent history and even within relatively short timeframes. The idea that human moral cognition is now rigidly fixed and constrained by traits forged during the Pleistocene—and that only supra-individual dynamics and processes drive significant moral change—appears empirically unsupported and inconsistent with available evidence. But what are the links between 'macro' and 'micro' levels, and how can we account for psychological moral change and increases in agency and open-ended reasoning abilities in naturalistic but non-deterministic terms?

Returning to Coleman's model, the evidence presented thus far seems to corroborate the lower-left part of the bath-tub model, specifically highlighting the presence and relevance of links 1 and 2 in the dynamics of moral change. However, this evidence does not yet conclusively disprove pure supra-individualist views. Although the evidence openly challenges the bold assertion that changes in individual psychology plays virtually *no role* in significant moral shifts (Sauer 2019; 2023; Smyth 2017; 2020), it can still be interpreted as compatible with a more charitable reading of a supra-individualist view, according to which psychological moral change is possible but only as a fortunate (and still limited) by-product of changes occurring at the macro level of socio-ecological conditions. If this moderate view were correct, it would still make little sense to prioritize intervention strategies focused on psychological change for achieving broader moral-social reforms at collective and institutional levels. My model challenges this weaker view as well. As we will see, micro-level psychological moral change is not merely an accidental by-product of supra-individual circumstances: under favorable conditions, it can be actively promoted and even catalyze socio-institutional moral change.[13]

The thesis I propose is relatively straightforward. Certain socio-ecological conditions can facilitate the acquisition of resources that can fenhance agency—defined as the increased ability to exert control over one's decisions, consider alternatives to prescribed or incentivized norms, and deviate from habits, traditions, learning histories, and biological pressures (the idea of 'open-ended normativity'). Christian Welzel identified several fundamental

---

13   It is important to avoid conflating the technical concept of an 'evolutionary by-product' with the notion of a 'by-product' as a secondary or incidental side-effect. In the former sense, the concept of an evolutionary by-product is not opposed to intentionality because intentionality is absent in the process of natural selection. A trait is considered an evolutionary by-product if it lacks a clear, direct biological function, yet its development can plausibly be explained as a consequence of other evolved traits. In the latter sense, however, understanding psychological and moral change as by-products of broader, supra-individual dynamics implies conceiving them as unintentional outcomes, explainable without invoking human moral agency, and essentially uncontrollable through interventions at the micro level of individual psychology. Here, I use the term 'by-product' in this second, more ordinary sense. Clarifying these two meanings is critical because the core thesis advanced here is twofold: (a) human moral cognition and the capacity for open-ended normativity can be understood as *evolutionary* by-products, while (b) specific instances of moral change as a mere by-product of unintentional supra-individual dynamics. These distinctions also concern different objects of analysis. On the one hand, I argue that human agency, moral cognition, and the capacity for open-ended normativity are best understood as evolutionary by-products; on the other hand, I contend that specific instances of moral change cannot be adequately explained as simple by-products of macro-level structural or institutional dynamics.

'action resources' that facilitate the rise of emancipative values and can enhance people's agency. These resources include material and social assets, intellectual and epistemic resources (e.g., greater access to information, formal education, and intellectual skills), and technologies and social conditions that facilitate their proliferation and stability (e.g., increased territorial and relational mobility, mass communication devices like the press or the Internet, and sufficient levels of freedom of association and expression) (Welzel 2013; Smyth 2020, 15-18; see also Buchanan 2020, 146). Such resources significantly expand the opportunities of individuals and institutions, enabling them to know, imagine, aspire to, and pursue new goals, courses of actions and ways of life, leading them to exert greater control over their lives, environments, and decisions.

These action resources facilitate open-ended moral reasoning and normativity, which involve the ability to critically evaluate received opinions, norms, and habits, and to consider and choose alternative courses of action that deviate from those immediately and strongly suggested and incentivized by specific types of learning and value representation (more on this below). Open-ended reasoning processes require costly resources,[14] but they enable the performance of unique of tasks and the establishment of distinctive institutions. Decades of research in cognitive (neuro)science show that moral (and non-moral) decisions can be modeled as the result of at least two types of learning and decision-making processes (Kahneman 2011; Greene 2014). While various dual-process frameworks exist in the literature, I rely here on the distinction, based on computational models of reinforcement learning, between model-free and model-based learning and decision-making algorithms (Bina 2022; Cushman 2013; Dolan & Dayan 2013; Greene 2017).

On the one hand, resources such as information and knowledge[15] facilitate model-based learning, reasoning, and decision-making,

---

14 Some of the most important ones include the availability of factual information and knowledge, as well as a diversity of social experiences, both of which are fundamental for developing reliable causal models of one's environment and envisioning possible alternative courses of action.

15 Here, I use 'knowledge' and 'information' in a broad sense, encompassing knowledge of (or information about) the likelihood that an event x occurs

which enhance agency and support *prospective* and *promotion-oriented* decision strategies. On the other hand, the absence of such resources and other socio-ecological conditions hinders open-ended reasoning and normativity, leading individuals to rely on model-free learning and decision-making processes, which in turn facilitate *retrospective* and *prevention-oriented* strategies (Welzel & Inglehart 2010, 49).

Fig. 1 *An evolutionary sequence of adaptive and open-ended links explaining increase in agency and open-ended normativity*

> 1.
> *Availability and environmental utility of resources (objective)*
>
> Socio-environmental conditions objectively define the opportunities available for survival and thriving.
>
> For example, in agrarian societies, attending formal education does not constitute opportunity to survive and thrive; in traditional patriarchal societies, professional training is not an opportunity for women's flourishing. As a result, institutions providing higher education or professional training for women are unlikely to emerge in such contexts (cf. the etiological theory of function). Their local absence further limits access to professional or academic education, reducing the chances of being directly or indirectly exposed to its benefits.

---

after y, as well as knowledge of (or information about) different points of view, reasons, and ways of living.

2.
Value utility (subjective)

People value, both individually and collectively is most advantageous given the opportunities available to them.

Under varying social, economic, cultural, or environmental conditions, certain resources and behaviors are valued and pursued more than others because they offer greater benefits for surviving and thriving, making them more accessible (less costly) and socially normalized (Bicchieri 2016). For instance, in agrarian societies, manual skills are typically very useful and, as a result, are more highly valued, pursued, and widespread compared to intellectual ones.

Differences in the objective utility and availability of resources (e.g., relational mobility, information, knowledge) shape how people value, pursue, and normalize different kinds of actions and behaviors. In market-integrated contexts, traits like tolerance and trust, openness to change, self-enhancement, self-actualization and self-expression are positively valued because they provide opportunities for thriving. Under different conditions (e.g., in less market-integrated societies), these traits are disvalued because they are useless, and can be even highly costly and dangerous, while traits such as conformity, defense of tradition, intensive kinship and stronger relational bonds are subjectively valued as they (objectively) provide greater opportunities to survive and thrive.

3.
Value representation – Pursuit strategies – Well-being link

When traits such as impersonal prosociality, knowledge, and emancipative values (e.g., self-actualization, self-enhancement, and self-expression) are valued and pursued due to their objective ecological utility, and when enabling resources are available, the conditions for greater agency and open-ended normativity are in place.
Impersonal prosociality fosters openness to new and alternative perspectives, ways of life, and norms. Knowledge and experience of different perspectives and alternative courses of actions, combined with increased analytic, prospective, and imaginative thinking, promotes model-based reasoning and decision-making (MB).

Traits such as self-actualization, self-enhancement, and self-expression are linked to lower levels of conformity to received norms and rituals, as well as greater decisional autonomy.
These traits, alongside altruism, are also considered to be among the highest sources of life satisfaction, which further incentivizes their development and pursuit.

While these traits are initially selected because they prove useful under specific conditions, they can later be repurposed for other goals. For instance, cognitive traits that evolved for other functions—such as enhanced analytic skills, mental time travel, and self-control—can facilitate more conscious and open-ended moral reasoning as by-products of their development.

Another way cognitive traits developed for other reasons can be used is engaging in more conscious and open-ended moral reasoning, enabled by model-based reasoning and decision-making, as a by-products of the selection of greater skills in some of its more specific components (e.g., greater analytic skills, mental time-travel, self-control, etc.) which originally evolved for other purposes.
Model-based reasoning relies on imagination and the ability to consider alternative possibilities using causal model (a mental 'map') of the environment, integrating representations of outcomes, expected values, and transition functions to guide decisions.

In contrast, a lack of resources, limited knowledge, and deferential values correlate with deontological and intuitive moral reasoning. Decisional inflexibility, static environments, and limited information favor model-free reasoning and decision-making (MF). MF operates by associating value to available actions based on past histories of rewards, without relying on a causal representation of the environment.

This model explains the increases in agency and open-ended normativity in recent history as by-products of the selection of psychological traits explainable by research such as Henrich's.[16]

---

16   Again, there is no reason to believe that moral agency and open-ended normativity depend on distinctively Western cognitive abilities. While these cognitive tendencies have been culturally prominent and highly

WEIRD psychological traits—such as analytic thinking, greater impersonal prosociality, and trust—facilitate engagement in more sophisticated model-based moral reasoning and decision-making, which are necessary for moral agency, open-ended normativity, and justification. Where the development of such psychological traits is advantageous—as in contexts of sociocultural exchange of material and epistemic goods—the impact of individual agency on social-institutional changes is greatest, because these changes are pursued more reflectively (though of course other non-agential causes and dynamics also play a role).

Conversely, where these traits are not favored—e.g., in contexts of poverty, isolation, or limited knowledge—parochialism, exclusivity, dogmatism, moral absolutism, and patriarchal values prevail. In such circumstances, individual decisions and behaviors are heavily shaped by tradition, social norms, taboos, fear, and deference to authority. As a result, psychological moral change struggles to drive socio-institutional moral change, because agency and open-ended normativity become more costly and constrained, while supra-individual socio-ecological causal dynamics gain prominence.

Under favorable circumstances, however, these traits can promote open-ended normativity, allowing individuals to become less dependent on their social contexts. While the development of specific psychological traits remain context-dependent, once these traits are developed, individuals gain greater freedom and control over their lives. They can imagine, represent, value, and pursue different goals and courses of action.

In such cases, macro-level social change is more significantly driven by individual action, with the bottom part of Coleman's bath-tub model carrying more explanatory weight:

> As an evolutionary process, value change involves humans as agents who make distinct strategy choices. Agency, understood as

---

valued in the West (partly due to the influence of technology and market economies), they are present across in all cultures and have been highly prized and developed in many of them. It's also worth noting that certain forms of model-based thinking (involved, for instance, in spatial navigation) are observed in other animals species, such as rodents.

the capacity to make purposeful choices, and the learning potential connected to agency, catapult the evolutionary pace of human societies on a new level, accelerating cultural evolution way beyond biological evolution (Welzel & Inglehart 2010, 46; see also Ayala 2010, 9019; Singer 1981/2011).

This model challenges Buchanan and Powell's claim that open-ended normativity and agency-driven 'inclusivist anomalies' cannot be explained in naturalistic, evolutionary terms.

6.
CAN TEACHING ETHICS FOSTER PSYCHOLOGICAL MORAL CHANGE?

6.1. *Recent moral anti-rationalism in moral psychology*

A final issue worth addressing concerns the idea—directly linked with the hard-wiring thesis and edorsed by both evo-conservatives and evo-liberals[1]—that traditional moral education (for example, through the teaching of ethics) is psychologically ineffective, particularly in the short term. I do not aim to provide a definitive answer to this complex problem here; however, I will offer some general reflections and discuss a few recent studies that point to a more optimistic view, though further comprehensive research remains necessary. As discussed at the beginning of the book, several scholars have recently argued that efforts to improve people's epistemic and moral capacities through traditional means (like education) are largely ineffective and likely doomed to failure (Haidt 2001; 2012; Persson & Savulescu 2017; 2019; Klenk & Sauer 2021; Levy 2021). Rather than promoting or improving people's reasoning and decision-making abilities by reducing biases, prejudices, or self-interested motivations, some scholars contend that it would be more effective to 'bypass' conscious reasoning by leveraging biases, heuristics, selfish motivations, and other cognitive limitations to achieve desired behavioral outcomes (Banaji & Greenwald 2013; Sauer 2019; Thaler & Sunstein 2008; Levy 2021).

Based on similar premises, a highly provocative yet influential proposal in contemporary applied ethicsadvocates for the development of biomedical moral enhancements (via drugs, genetic manipulation, or neural implants). Proponents argue that

---

1   For a discussion of these positions, see chapter 2 of this volume.

such interventions are necessary to address humanity's most urgent and complex moral problems, given that ordinary means of moral education and reform are insufficient to produce significant psychological, epistemic, and behavioral change (Douglas 2008; Persson & Savulescu 2008; 2012).

The question of whether moral reasoning can influence moral psychology and behavior lies at the heart of a long-standing debate in both philosophy and psychology. While moral reasoning has traditionally been considered crucial for guiding decisions, recent research—most notably that of Haidt (2001; 2012)—suggests that reasoning about moral issues primarily functions as post hoc rationalization for actions driven by more automatic, emotionally-based, instinctive processes, i.e., our hard-wired moral psychology. The effectiveness of ethics education, therefore, hinges on addressing this fundamental question: if reasoning cannot drive moral change, does ethics hold any practical utility?

Historically, moral philosophy has emphasized the importance of rational deliberation for living and acting well. Many classical thinkers and philosophical traditions have argued that reason is not only essential to guide one's moral decisions and to build one's character (Hadot 1995; Ivanhoe 2000; Kant 1785/1996; Mill 1859/2003). In the past, as well as today, many scholars have argued that reasoning plays a significant role not only in retrospectively justifying moral decisions, but also in guiding future judgments and actions. However, this traditional view has faced substantial challenges in recent decades, especially from researchers in moral psychology. A growing body of empirical evidence suggests that moral reasoning may not be the primary driver of ethical decisions. Instead, intuition and emotion appear to play a much larger role in shaping judgments and behavior (Haidt 2001; 2012; Prinz 2007). Moral reasoning, in this view, essentially serves the post hoc function of rationalizing decisions that were made intuitively rather than through deliberate thought. This shift in understanding raises critical questions about the role and efficacy of ethics education: if moral reasoning is secondary to intuition and emotion, can teaching and reflecting on ethical issues have any practical implication?

Moral reasoning, in its traditional sense, refers to the conscious, reflective process by which individuals deliberate on ethical questions, weighing principles such as justice, fairness, consequences, and the prevention of harm. This deliberative process has historically been considered a hallmark of moral decision-making and the focus of much ethics education, which encourages individuals to engage in careful reflection when faced with moral dilemmas. Throughout much of the 20th century, the development of moral reasoning was seen as essential to moral development. Among the earliest and most influential theories in moral psychology in the second half of the 20th century was that of Lawrence Kohlberg (1981; 1984), who believed that ontogenetic moral development depends on the emergence of increasingly sophisticated reasoning abilities. Kohlberg proposed stage-based model of moral development in which individuals advance from a pre-conventional focus on personal consequences to post-conventional reasoning grounded in universal ethical principles such as justice and human rights. Kohlberg placed reason at the center of moral development, assuming that, as individuals moved through these stages, they would make better moral decisions. This rationalist approach heavily influenced the teaching of ethics, where the goal was to cultivate an individual's capacity to engage in higher-level moral reasoning through education and reflection.

Despite the dominance of this rationalist paradigm, more recent research has cast doubt on the causal role of moral reasoning in ethical decision-making. One of the most influential challenges comes from Jonathan Haidt's *social intuitionist model*, which suggests that moral judgments are primarily the product of automatic, emotional processes (which in turn are produced by the activation of evolved 'social receptors' or 'modules' in the moral mind, selected over millennia for their adaptiveness to fundamental socio-environmental challenges). Individuals often make moral judgments intuitively, guided by emotional responses, with reasoning entering only later to rationalize these intuitive decisions.

This model has significant implications for how we approach the teaching of ethics and moral reflection more broadly. If moral judgments are primarily driven by emotional and intuitive processes rather than reflective reasoning, traditional approaches to moral education and decision-making emphasizing rational deliberation may have limited effectiveness in producing meaningful change. Haidt's findings align with a broader body of research highlighting the role of emotion and intuition in moral cognition. Based on (or alongside) this skepticism regarding the role of reasoning in moral psychology, other authors have argued that alternative processes and dynamics are more common and effective in promoting moral change. These include affective reinforcement learning, where individuals modify their behavior based on feedback (rewards and punishments) from their environment, and motivated reasoning, where judgments are shaped by emotions and desires rather than by neutral reflection (Kunda 1990; Campbell & Kumar 2012). Additionally, research on moral exemplars, such as Zagzebski's work (2017), suggests that individuals are often more influenced by admiration and imitation of virtuous role models than by reasoning alone. This focus on emotions is reflected in some recent neo-Aristotelian approaches to character education, which aim to shape moral behavior more directly by fostering virtue and emotional learning in young children, rather than prioritizing the development of more general reasoning skills about ethical matters. (Kristjánsson 2007; 2015).

6.2. *Teaching ethics can foster behavior change*

Despite this skepticism regarding the role of reasoning in morality, a recently replicated study conducted in the United States found that participation in ethics classes (optionally combined with documentary videos), can influence people's behavior on morally significant issues, such as reducing meat consumption (see Schwitzgebel et al. 2020; 2023). Specifically, the authors tested whether discussing the ethical implications of meat production could lead to changes in students' dietary choices. This study contributes to the broader debate on the effectiveness of moral reasoning in driving behavioral change, especially in contexts where reasoning about moral issues such as animal welfare and environmental concerns intersects with everyday habits like eating.

The researchers used an experimental design involving two groups of students: one discussed ethical issues related to meat consumption, while a control group focused on the ethics of charity. The study measured changes in meat consumption before and after the intervention. Students exposed to ethical arguments about eating meat reported a significant reduction in meat consumption compared to the control group (regardless of whether they watched optional videos). This suggests that engaging in moral reasoning about specific ethical issues can influence behavior, even months after the intervention (see Schwitzgebel et al. 2020; 2023). Students confronted with ethical arguments against meat consumption may have experienced discomfort if their behavior did not align with the ethical considerations they had encountered and reflected on. To resolve this cognitive dissonance, students may have opted to change their behavior by reducing their meat consumption, rather than rejecting the ethical principles they recognized as valid.

The study shows that moral reasoning is not merely post-hoc rationalization but can function as a driver of behavioral change. This suggests that the dichotomy between reasoning and intuition may not be as stark as Haidt's model implies. Instead, there may be a more complex interplay between reasoning, emotion, and behavior. The students in the meat ethics group may have experienced emotional reactions to the ethical arguments they encountered, which in turn could have prompted them to reflect more deeply on their dietary habits and led them to change their behavior (Sauer 2017).

The results of the study have important implications for the design and implementation of ethics education programs. If moral reasoning can indeed lead to behavioral changes in areas such as meat consumption, ethics education could become a powerful tool for fostering reflective behavior change on a broader scale. By pushing people to reflect on the inconsistencies between their beliefs and their actions, moral reasoning can help them become more aware of their own moral inconsistencies and motivate them to change their behavior. This approach could be particularly effective in fostering behavioral changes related to challenges such as social and global inequalities, sustainability, public health, animal welfare, and many, where conflicts between habits and moral principles often arise.

While the study just discussed offers valuable insights into how teaching ethics and moral reasoning might influence behavior, it has significant limitations that merit careful consideration. One major limitation lies in the type of moral change the researchers evaluated. They focused on measuring how closely participants' behavior aligned with a specific outcome—in this case, a reduction in meat consumption (for a critique, see Songhorian et al. 2022). This method fails to consider changes in more general moral reasoning skills, such as the ability to analyze and comprehend moral dilemmas, or the capacity to justify one's decisions. In philosophical discussions, these skills are often seen as essential components of moral agency. A purely behavioral reduction in meat consumption, while ethically significant, represents just one facet of moral action, and does not capture other important elements of moral change.

Furthermore, certain moral issues, like meat consumption, are relatively straightforward and uncontroversial, at least within philosophical debates. Reducing meat consumption is widely regarded as morally good due to concerns about animal welfare, environmental sustainability, and health. However, many moral issues are far more complex and controversial, requiring greater flexibility and nuance in moral reasoning. For example, moral dilemmas involving trade-offs between different values—such as privacy vs. security, or individual rights vs. collective welfare—demand a more sophisticated ability to navigate competing ethical principles. An educational approach that measures improvement solely by compliance with predefined outcomes might fail to equip individuals to grapple with such complexities (Songhorian et al. 2022).

Additionally, this approach risks turning moral education into a form of indoctrination indoctrination, leading students to uncritically adopt specific moral positions uncritically. This concern arises if ethics courses overemphasize the moral correctness of certain outcomes without encouraging students to critically evaluate different moral perspectives. Moral education should avoid simply imposing a particular moral viewpoint, as this undermines the development of autonomous moral agency. If students reduce their meat consumption primarily because they are emotionally moved by disturbing images of animal suffering—rather than because they have engaged in thoughtful moral reasoning—their behavior may reflect conditioning rather than genuine moral understanding (Songhorian et al. 2022). In Bina (2022) and Bina et al. (2024), I highlighted the importance of cultivating flexibility in moral reasoning as opposed to merely educating intuitions or emotional responses according to predetermined theoretical standards, such as a specific normative framework.

6.3 *Teaching ethics can foster change in moral reasoning and justification abilities*

Another—complementary—approach may involve observing changes in people's abilities for moral reasoning and justification of moral decisions, rather than focusing solely on behavioral outputs such as those observed by Schwitzgebel and colleagues (for a critique, see Bina 2024c). How can one measure shifts in people's abilities to reason morally and handle complex moral decisions? This is a critical issue in moral psychology. The current section explores a procedural, non-substantive approach to evaluating such changes and emphasizes how it differs from traditional models.

An alternative to observing moral change based merely on behavioral outcomes consists in focusing on individuals' abilities to offer moral justifications for their choices. Hence, the aim is not to determine whether individuals arrive at a 'correct' moral conclusion but rather to evaluate the quality of reasoning and justification employed when navigating morally complex situations. What distinguishes this approach is that it is not interested primarily in what individuals do, judge, or believe, but in the processes through which they reach their conclusions, and in the abilities to provide reasons and justifications to support their actions, judgments, and beliefs: in this framework, moral change can be observed by looking at shifts in *how* a moral conclusion is reached and justified, rather than focusing exclusively on the conclusion itself. Together with a team of colleagues at San Raffaele University in Milan, I developed a framework to evaluate people's justification abilities based on the following features (Songhorian et al. 2022; cf. Schaefer & Savulescu 2019):

- *Logical competence*, i.e., the ability to make correct logical inferences, identify inconsistencies in one's and others' judgements, and recognize the implications of one's beliefs and the matter of contention between interlocutors;[2]
- *Conceptual understanding*, i.e., a grasp of the content and scope of application of moral concepts and ideas, and the ability to communicate it clearly (Schafer & Savulescu 2019, 77; see also Moody-Adams 1999);
- *Empirical competence*, i.e., knowledge of non-moral, empirical facts;[3]

---

2   "One might hold, for instance, the following three views: all corrupt politicians should be punished no matter how mild the corruption; one's favourite politician is mildly corrupt; and one's favourite politician should not be punished for so mild a corruption, given all the good work she is doing. These are jointly inconsistent, as the first two views imply by modus ponens that one's favourite politician should be punished even for mild corruption. Something has to give—logically, one of the views must be given up" (Schaefer & Savulescu 2019, 76).

3   Consider this argument proposed as an example by Schaefer and Savulescu:
    "P1: Senator Barney accepts bribes
    P2: Anyone accepting bribes should be punished
    C: Senator Barney should be punished
    P2 and the conclusion are moral claims, and so without further elaboration are untouched by empirical concerns. However, P1 is an empirical, non-moral claim. The moral conclusion only follows if it is correct. Anyone endorsing the conclusion that Senator Barney should be punished on the basis of the above reasoning needs to have good grounds for the claim that Senator Barney accepts bribes. Some sort of evidence such as a witness of the bribery will be needed. And those evaluating such evidence

- *Openness to the revision* of one's opinions;
- *Empathic understanding*, i.e., the ability to consider and understand others' situation (Schaefer & Savulescu 2019, 79);
- *Bias avoidance*, i.e., the ability to recognize and mitigate the influence of irrelevant factors in moral judgments.[4]

I will not discuss and justify each of these requirements in detail here (for discussion, see Schaefer and Savulescu 2019), and this list should be understood as partial and open to revision. However, I believe it represents a promising example of how such evaluations could and should proceed. A procedural account like this enables a more neutral and pluralistic approach, "thus avoiding many question-begging moral assumptions" (Schaefer & Savulescu 2019, 75). Many moral disputes are so controversial that it is problematic to claim that there is one single true or correct solution, that everyone has reasons to accept.

But how can we ensure that such a procedural account of moral justification can distinguish reflective, reason-driven moral change from post-hoc rationalization of intuitions or emotions (Haidt 2001; 2012)? First, the emphasis on logical coherence and conceptual competence and clarity ensures that justifications must adhere to rational standards. This prevents individuals from relying solely on rhetorical strategies if their arguments lack logical soundness. Second, individuals may provide justifications that include reasons that were part of their decision-making process. Although Haidt (2001) suggests that moral reasoning often occurs as a post hoc rationalization for emotional responses, this does not imply that

---

will need to assess a number of factors. Is the witness reliable? How do we know what was witnessed was really a bribe? What did the briber procure? Those who are generally more competent at evaluating empirical claims will more reliably ascertain the truth of P1, and in turn make more reliable evaluations of the moral question of whether Senator Barney should be punished" (Schaefer & Savulescu 2019, 77).

4   For example, "how you frame a question should not matter to one's opinion of it; one should not hold oneself to different moral standards as that of others; one should not privilege one's relations over others in the public sphere; and so on" (ibid., 81)

people cannot align their justificatory reasons with considerations that were involved in their reasoning process prior to the decision (ex ante) (Songhorian et al., 2022). In fact, people are capable of reflecting on their judgments and offering justifications consistent with their earlier reasoning processes, even if those reasons are disclosed only after the decision has been made.

Drawing on empirical research, Haidt concludes that moral judgment is not the product of conscious reasoning, but the expression of automatic, unconscious, and affectively-laden 'intuitions' shaped by evolutionary, cultural, and social pressures. Within this model, conscious reasoning intervenes only ex post by concocting reasons to support and socially justify fast and automatic reactions: "one feels a quick flash of revulsion [...] and knows intuitively that something is wrong. Then, when faced with a social demand for a verbal justification, one becomes a lawyer trying to build a case rather than a judge searching for the truth" (Haidt 2001, 182). According to Haidt, the function of moral reasoning is to socially justify intuitive responses, but it has no causal power in shaping their content ex ante. In this framework, increased proficiency in the ability to provide socially acceptable justifications would merely enhance the ability to persuade others of the acceptability of conclusions that are remain essentially impervious to rational scrutiny and revision.

However, certain reasons or justifications can be more consistent, more responsive to empirical evidence and others' perspectives, reasons and interests, and more open to revision than others. Such justifications do not merely confirm one's opinions, intuitions, or feelings by effectively convincing other people (and perhaps even oneselves) of their acceptability; they also express the effort of considering a broader spectrum of information, such as non-moral facts, or the interests and preferences of the individuals involved (including those of the agent). If Schaefer and Savulescu's criteria are reasonable, one can discriminate between confabulations, motivated or confirmatory rationalizations, and reflective moral justifications.

In light of Haidt's work, a confabulation can be understood as the attempt to fabricate justifications for moral conclusions often resulting in clear logical fallacies or contradictions, pushed by the desire to hold and confirm one's intuitive judgments and beliefs even when faced with inconsistencies or contrasting rational arguments (Festinger 1957; Kunda 1990). In Haidt's famous experiments, some participants try to rustle up support for their intuitive conclusions by offering fallacious and motivated justifications that either clash with relevant information or merely restate their intuitive conclusions without justifying them at all (Haidt 2001; 2012). Therefore, we can conceive confabulation as a kind of reason-giving that lacks several features of a reflective, or reason-driven justification (such as empirical and logical consistency, and openness to revision).

Rationalization can be conceived, more broadly, as the justification of a behavioral output by offering reasons in its support "that would have made it rational" (Cushman 2020, 183), even if such reasons do not reflect the actual decision-making process that led to that output. Many rationalizations can be more consistent and sensitive to logical reasoning and evidence than moral confabulations. However, providing reasons in favor of a moral judgment does not guarantee that these reasons constitute reason-driven moral justifications, because what is rational, e.g., from a self-interested point of view may not be so from a moral point of view. For example, a rationalization may be grounded on an astute selection of data, aimed to make the preferred conclusion plausible, whereas a reason-driven moral justification does consider a broader range of morally relevant factors, such as the interests of other individuals involved. Moreover, even though rationalization requires paying attention to possible influences of biases on argumentation, it does not require taking seriously, for instance, the main moral reasons for and against available options or courses of action. Supporting moral conclusions with reason-driven moral justifications does not simply require a generic capacity to provide any kind of reasons in their favor, but a much more specific kind of reason-giving account.[5]

Reflective moral justifications, thus, require adequately understanding the context of the situation under evaluation,

---

5   Thanks to Massimo Reichlin for helping me articulate this distinction between confabulation, rationalization, and reason-driven moral justification in these terms.

including one's own and others' perspectives. Reflective justifications balance reasons for and against various conclusions in light of available information, showing the attitude to evaluate potential alternatives with an open mind, and a willingness to reconsider one's opinions. The potential influences of biases or prejudices that might affect the evaluation are also taken into account in reflective moral justifications. Such justifications avoid considering one's preferences as the right evaluative standard for the situation at hand, acknowledging and balancing the different interests at stake. Reflective moral justifications also tend to satisfy standards of logical consistency. Improving in these capacities does not simply mean improving the ability to justify any possible moral judgment or behavior—as the objection I am addressing states—because if these conditions are met, the range of reasonable (or potentially acceptable) moral conclusions narrows significantly.

A notable strenght of this approach is that it remains valid even if Haidt's model of moral judgment is correct. Even if in isolated, specific circumstances of choice, explicit moral reasoning only intervenes after quicker psychological responses, changes in justificatory abilities would not just support a-rational outputs, but can be sensitive to independent relevant information. Nonetheless, there are several reasons to challenge Haidt's thesis according to which moral reasoning has no causal influence over moral intuitions and judgments. Several critics have challenged Haidt's rigid dichotomy between controlled and automatic processes, as well as his neglect of the diachronic dimension of moral judgment (Campbell & Kumar 2012; Railton 2014). Even if it does not come into play immediately before the expression of a moral conclusion at the time of decision, explicit moral reasoning can feedback on and inform people's future moral responses (Sauer 2017). If this is accurate, moral justifications can also reliably point out some of the reasons that informed one's intuitive judgment or behavior (Cushman 2020), a feature absent in motivated (or confirmatory) rationalizations. Reflective moral justifications can be distinguished from other reason-giving accounts. By distinguishing reflective moral justifications from other forms of reason-giving, we can counter the objection that procedural views merely recognize rhetorical improvements in rationalizing as instances of reason-driven moral change. In conclusion, the procedural method suggested here offers a straightforward framework for identifying reason-driven moral change, as well as for its implementation and measurement.

A key methodological distinction between the procedural approach to measuring moral reasoning and traditional Kohlbergian or neo-Kohlbergian frameworks lies in how changes in moral reasoning are evaluated. Kohlberg and his successors typically used structured, closed-ended questions to assess individuals' moral development, focusing on responses that correspond to predefined stages of moral reasoning (Rest et al., 1999; Thoma, 2014). In contrast, the procedural approach emphasizes open-ended questions, which allow for a more flexible exploration of how participants reason through complex ethical situations without being guided toward particular answers. In Kohlberg's model, moral reasoning is assessed through a stage-based framework. Each participant's moral reasoning is classified based on the moral stage their responses align with, progressing from self-interest to higher-level ethical principles such as justice. This method uses dilemma-based questionnaires where participants select from a range of predetermined responses, which are then used to evaluate their moral maturity. Although this model provides insight into developmental patterns, it is limited by its reliance on closed-ended questions that offer pre-set moral options (Rest et al., 1999).

In contrast, the procedural approach that we used avoids imposing such structured pathways, as it does not seek to map individuals' reasoning onto pre-defined stages of moral development. Instead, it allows for a more open-ended evaluation of moral reasoning, which encourages participants to articulate their thought processes without being constrained by pre-packaged answers. Our procedural approach evaluates moral change by focusing on how individuals justify their decisions in morally complex scenarios. The use of open-ended questions encourages participants to engage in spontaneous moral reasoning, providing richer data about their ethical thinking. This contrasts with Kohlberg's structured tests, where participants' responses are often limited to selecting among pre-defined moral judgments.

To further understand how ethics education might influence moral reasoning, at San Raffaele University in Milan we conducted a controlled experimental study designed to evaluate whether a brief intervention, like a single lesson on moral reasoning, could result in changes in individuals' abilities to provide moral justifications when faced with complex ethical dilemmas. Participants were recruited based on specific inclusion criteria (e.g., ensuring that no prior philosophical training influenced their moral reasoning abilities. We excluded individuals with a background in philosophical studies, as their previous training might have influenced their ability to engage with the task in ways not representative of the general population). 65 students underwent an initial neuropsychological screening to assess their abstract reasoning, empathy, and mood. This screening process allowed us to control for cognitive and emotional factors that could affect moral reasoning independently of the intervention.

Students were asked to engage with a complex moral dilemma, and the task was specifically designed to prevent any option from being deemed objectively 'correct' or preferred; the focus was on observing the reasoning process rather than pushing participants toward a particular moral conclusion. After making their decision, participants were required to justify their choice through an open-ended response. The purpose of the task was to stimulate ethical reasoning and evaluate how participants articulated their moral justifications, without guiding them toward a particular moral philosophy (e.g., consequentialism vs. deontology). The study involved two groups: a control group and an experimental group, each exposed to different interventions designed to stimulate reasoning—either logical or moral.

In the non-moral (control) group, participants attended an introductory class on logical reasoning, consisting of a brief text followed by a 75-minute lecture. The lesson focused on general principles of logical argumentation, covering essential topics such as deduction, induction, abduction, refutation, semantic fallacy, petitio principii. In the moral (experimental) group, participants attended an introductory class on moral reasoning, consisting of a brief text followed by a 75-minute lecture. This intervention focused on relevant factors for any normative ethical theory, including consequences, rights, rules, fairness, merit, and responsibility. Participants had to answer the same dilemma and justify their answer before the intervention (pre-test), immediately after (post-test) and one month later (follow up). Participants' justifications for their decisions were analyzed using a qualitative coding framework. We developed a six-criteria procedural model to evaluate participants' moral reasoning, based on Schaefer & Savulescu's framework outlined above:

1. Empirical Competence: How well does the participant identify and incorporate relevant non-moral facts into their moral reasoning?
2. Conceptual Competence: Does the participant use ethical concepts (e.g., rights, fairness, consequences) accurately and appropriately?
3. Logical Coherence: Is the participant's reasoning internally consistent, without contradictions?
4. Openness to Revision: Does the participant demonstrate flexibility in their judgment, showing a willingness to reconsider or modify their stance when confronted with new information or perspectives?
5. Sympathetic Imagination: Does the participant show an ability to engage with the perspectives of others and consider how their decisions affect different individuals?
6. Bias Reduction: To what extent does the participant detect or try to reduce personal biases?

Each participant's response was evaluated on these six dimensions, with each criterion being scored on a 0-2 scale:

0   Absent or entirely lacking in the participant's response.
1   Implicitly present or weakly developed.
2   Explicitly present and well developed.

Three independent evaluators were tasked with assessing the participants' responses. The evaluators were blind to which group each participant belonged to (control or experimental).

I will briefly discuss the key findings of our study (still unpublished)[6] and provide a deeper analysis of the implications for understanding the role of teaching ethics for psychological change.

Participants in the moral reasoning condition exhibited notable change in both conceptual competence ($p = 0.007$) and logical coherence ($p = 0.023$) immediately after the intervention, with these changes sustained over time. Students exposed to the moral reasoning intervention demonstrated a clear change in their ability to articulate moral concepts. These changes were observed immediately after the intervention and persisted to some degree at the follow-up stage one month later ($p = 0.013$), although the effect had diminished slightly by this point ($p = 0.032$). The sustained increase suggests that moral reasoning interventions can lead to meaningful change in participants' ability to reason and express themselves about moral issues, even if the benefits wane slightly over time. Logical coherence also showed significant change in the moral group, both immediately after the intervention and at the follow-up. Unlike conceptual competence, there was no significant drop in logical coherence between the post-intervention and follow-up, indicating that participants retained the ability to organize their arguments in a logically consistent way. The consistency of this finding suggests that teaching moral reasoning may provide participants with a stronger framework for maintaining logical rigor in their moral justifications compared to an intervention on non-moral reasoning and argumentation. Our findings suggest that teaching moral reasoning, even in a short-term intervention, can have a lasting impact on certain key reasoning skills, particularly in helping individuals maintain logical coherence in their moral deliberations.

One notable trend across both the moral and non-moral groups was the general decline in reasoning abilities observed at the follow-up stage, particularly with respect to the less tangible dimensions of reasoning, such as sympathetic imagination, openness to revision,

---

6   See Bina et al. (unpublished manuscript).

and bias reduction. These skills were generally weakly developed in both groups and did not show any significant improvement, either immediately after the intervention or at the follow-up.

Sympathetic imagination and bias reduction remained largely underexpressed. This finding is consistent with previous research indicating that fostering sympathetic imagination and reducing bias in moral reasoning are particularly challenging to achieve in short-term interventions. This suggests that longer or more targeted interventions may be required to produce significant changes in these competences.

While both groups showed some degree of improvement immediately after the intervention, the moral reasoning group outperformed the logical reasoning group in several key areas, particularly in conceptual competence and logical coherence. The moral group's superior performance on these dimensions points to the effectiveness of moral reflection in helping individuals develop more nuanced and conceptually sound justifications for their moral decisions. However, the general decline in reasoning abilities at the follow-up stage in both groups suggests that repeated or more comprehensive interventions may be necessary to ensure the long-term retention of these skills.

It is important to note that the follow-up was conducted online; the less controlled environment of an online setting could have influenced participants' responses in various ways, and participants may have been less engaged with the task. Overall, our findings suggest that teaching moral reasoning can have a meaningful impact on participants' ability to reason about moral issues and to justify their moral decisions, particularly with respect to conceptual competence and logical coherence. Our findings support the broader argument that moral education, when properly structured, can provide individuals with the conceptual tools and argumentative skills necessary to engage more thoughtfully with complex moral dilemmas.

In conclusion, this study shows that just one ethics lesson can have significant effects on reasoning abilities, contrary to what many recent criticisms have argued. The study's limitations and time constraints (one lesson is obviously not enough) suggest that further investigation is needed. However, the results are already encouraging and suggest that teaching ethics is not entirely useless; significant changes can be achieved even in a very short time, as with just one class. Together with the study by Schwitzgebel and colleagues, which shows that ethics classes can produce significant behavioral changes, there is reason to believe that teaching ethics can lead to meaningful changes (even over a short timeframe) in how individuals respond to urgent and novel challenges, that our psychology has not has not been adapted to face for most of our of evolutionary history. This finding challenges the evo-conservative and evo-liberal assumption that moral education is useless and ineffective for addressing pressing contemporary moral issues.

CONCLUSIONS

The idea that moral psychology, behavior, norms, and beliefs are direct products of evolution by natural selection has received increased attention and support over the past few decades. Many scientists and philosophers believe that these aspects of morality were selected in human populations because of their contribution to increasing chances of survival and reproduction. This book outlined and critically analyzed this research program and the arguments offered by its proponents, evaluating its robustness by discussing several scientific and philosophical works. Empirical evidence and more fundamental theoretical considerations show that the idea that morality and moral psychology are direct products of natural selection is poorly grounded. I have thus highlighted some important implications for several proposals (theoretical and practical) that have been recently defended in light of evolutionary explanations of human cognition and morality.

Within recent scientific and philosophical debates, many scholars have claimed that human psychology and morality are strongly constrained by our evolutionary history, especially by the environmental and social challenges that our ancestors had to face for millennia (Curry 2016; Greene 2013; Haidt 2012; Joyce 2006; Street 2006; Tomasello & Vaish 2013; cf. Buchanan & Powell 2015; 2018; Buchanan 2020). Proponents of this view have claimed that selective pressures since the late Pleistocene in the advent of modernity favored a psychology that was adaptive for pre-modern environments and small societies, which still significantly influences moral cognition, beliefs, and behaviors today. The product of this selective process is, they argue, a tribalistic, exclusivist, and short-sighted psychology which, according to the more radical versions of this view, is doomed to remain the same, or at least it would require millennia of evolution to change: traits take millennia to evolve, ordinary means and projects for moral and epistemic improvement are too slow compared to the speed of social and techno-scientific development. Consequently, traditional means for moral change prove ineffective in addressing the vast cooperative and existential challenges posed by contemporary phenomena such as anthropogenic climate change, mass migrations, global inequalities, the risks of artificial intelligence, and more.

This work primarily investigated the scientific validity of this thesis rather than focusing on its ethical or political implications. In particular, the volume examined and challenged two main ideas: (i) the idea that morality, and especially human moral psychology, is a direct product of natural selection; and (ii) the idea that today, human psychology and moral systems (of norms and beliefs) are still heavily influenced by the evolutionary history of our species, to the point that it is impossible or at least very hard to change them. The conclusion of this book is that the view that human psychology and morality are essentially and rigidly limited because of their evolutionary history is not supported by scientific and philosophical research on the subject. Significant psychological and moral changes appear, on the contrary, to be possible—even within relatively short timeframes.

An objection that could be raised against the conclusions presented in this book is that they are overly optimistic, utopian, and based on wishful thinking. Skeptics might argue that the evidence and arguments that have been offered here merely that human beings possess the capacity to be more prosocial, cooperative, trusting, universalist, farsighted, and to broaden their circle of moral concern beyond their narrow social groups, to change their behavior and their conceptual and reasoning abilities through ethical reflection. However, they might argue, this does not show that significant moral change—significant *enough* to successfully tackle the most pressing cooperative problems of our time—is actually occurring. Even if people are becoming more inclusivist, fair, trusting, universalist, caring about animals and future generations (and so forth) than before, skeptics might argue that this may not suffice to address immense challenges like climate change. For example, although many people may endorse the idea of equal moral worth of every human being, their behavior often does not align with these values, nor it is sufficient to address complex systemic problems like global poverty.

These concerns are perfectly understandable and should be taken seriously. However, the conclusions of the analysis conducted in this book should not be interpreted as asserting that psychological change is the only solution to complex cooperative problems, which must also—and likely primarily—be addressed on institutional and political levels. There is certainly a relationship between the two dimensions, and I have sought to show that psychological dispositions, beliefs, and values that are more flexible, attentive, sensitive, and motivated toward the interests, rights, freedoms, and well-being of excluded, oppressed, and most vulnerable most vulnerable subjects also facilitate the establishment and functioning of institutions capable of addressing those issues more systemically. Second, the main argument presented here was intended to counter the claim that humanity is essentially constrained by a rigid tribalistic and biased moral psychology that also prevents the realization of those very institutional responses; or, alternatively, that inclusivist, cooperative and farsighted institutional responses can only succeed by leveraging hard-wired biases and self-interested motivations, as some scholars have suggested. On the contrary, I have shown that a more inclusivist, forward-looking, prosocial and less-biased psychology can help create and sustain more inclusive, cooperative, and forward-looking institutions.

There is also significant evidence and counterarguments to the objection that this change appears to occur only in theory and not in practice, some of which have been extensively discussed. A clear example is the notable shift in attitudes and behaviors toward social norms discriminating and oppressing women, members of the LGBTQIA+ community, ethnic minorities, and people with disabilities in the direction of greater equality, inclusion, and respect; toward the sustainability of our productive and economic systems and lifestyles, and their impact on ecosystems and populations already affected by neocolonialism and anthropogenic climate change; attitudes, beliefs, and behaviors towards distant individuals in severely unfortunate conditions have shifted dramatically in recent years; powerful and functioning institutions actively implement these values and other universalist and cosmopolitan moral principles, such as international and regional human rights systems and development programs; attitudes and behaviors, as well as laws, aimed at protecting ecosystems and non-human animal species have drastically changed in recent years. And the list could continue.

A further and final objection may be that even if expanding our circle of moral concern to encompass all humanity, nature, and future beings is possible, in practice it would be overly demanding. However, the possibility of being more attentive and actively respecting subjects worthy of moral consideration does not necessarily conflict with pursuing personal goals and living a good and satisfying life. As anthropological, sociological and psychological research widely show, high levels of prosociality positively correlate with individual well-being and life satisfaction. Moreover, norms, institutions and division of labor can make it perfectly feasible to comply with universalist and egalitarian principles and norms simply by doing one's part within a larger cooperative system (by respecting and supporting inclusivist norms and institutions) without having to actively empathize with, or directly help, all humanity and sentient beings on the planet. This approach to morality, which depends on an expanded set of experiences and knowledge, on the awareness of being part of a broader system of relationships, on the consideration of the wider-reaching effects of one's actions, on the respect of universalist principles, and trust in institutions is made easier precisely by the psychological changes toward greater impersonal prosociality discussed throughout this volume. These changes enable people to emancipate themselves from strong, spatially and culturally limited, biased, and exclusivist social and traditional bonds, opening up to a broader consideration of the impact that our actions and lives can have on all the subjects deserving moral consideration and respect.

REFERENCES

Aarøe, L., Petersen, M. B., Arceneaux, K. (2017). The behavioral immune system shapes political intuitions: Why and how individual differences in disgust sensitivity underlie opposition to immigration. American Political Science Review, 111(2), 277-294.

Aksoy, C. G., Carpenter, C. S., De Haas, R., Tran, K. D. (2020). Do laws shape attitudes? Evidence from same-sex relationship recognition policies in Europe. European Economic Review, 124, 103399.

Alexander, R. D. (1987/2017). The biology of moral systems. Routledge.

Algoe, S. B., Haidt, J. (2009). Witnessing excellence in action: The 'other-praising' emotions of elevation, gratitude, and admiration. Journal of Positive Psychology 4(2), 105-127.

Allport, G. (1954). The nature of prejudice. Addison-Wesley.

Andrews, K. (2020). The animal mind: An introduction to the philosophy of animal cognition. Routledge.

Arnhart, L. (2005). Darwinian conservatism. Imprint Academic.

Arvan, M. (2021). Morality as an evolutionary exaptation. In J. De Smedt, H. De Cruz (eds.). Empirically engaged evolutionary ethics. Springer, 89-109.

Arvan, M. (2019). The dark side of morality: Group polarization and moral epistemology. In The Philosophical Forum, 50, 1, 87-115.

Asch, S. E. (1956). Studies of independence and conformity: I. A minority of one against a unanimous majority. Psychological Monographs: General and Applied, 70(9), 1-70.

Asma, S. T. (2012). Against fairness. University of Chicago Press.

Awad, E., Dsouza, S., Shariff, A., Rahwan, I., Bonnefon, J. F. (2020). Universals and variations in moral decisions made in 42 countries by 70,000 participants. Proceedings of the National Academy of Sciences, 117(5), 2332-2337.

Axelrod, R. (1984). The evolution of cooperation. Basic Books.

Ayala, F. (2010). The difference of being human: Morality. Proceedings of the National Academy of Sciences, 107(2), 9015-9022.

Bago, B., De Neys, W. (2019). The intuitive greater good: Testing the corrective dual process model of moral cognition. Journal of Experimental Psychology: General, 148(10).

Banaji, M. R., Greenwald, A. G. (2013). Blind spot: Hidden biases of good people. Delacorte.

Barclay, P. (2016). Biological markets and the effects of partner choice on cooperation and friendship. Current opinion in psychology, 7, 33-38.

Barclay, P., Willer, R. (2007). Partner choice creates competitive altruism in humans. Proceedings of the Royal Society B: Biological Sciences, 274(1610), 749-753.

Barkow, J. H., Cosmides, L., Tooby, J. (eds.). (1995). The adapted mind: Evolutionary psychology and the generation of culture. Oxford University Press.

Barrett, H. C., Bolyanatz, A., Crittenden, A. N., Fessler, D. M., Fitzpatrick, S., Gurven, M., Henrich, J., Kanovsky, M., Kushnick, A., Scelza, B. A., Stich, S., von Rueden, C., Zhao, W., Laurence, S. (2016). Small-scale societies exhibit fundamental variation in the role of intentions in moral judgment. Proceedings of the National Academy of Sciences, 113(17), 4688-4693.

Baumard, N., André, J. B., Sperber, D. (2013). A mutualistic approach to morality: The evolution of fairness by partner choice. Behavioral and Brain Sciences, 36(1), 59-78.

Bennis, W. M., Medin, D. L., Bartels, D. M. (2010). The costs and benefits of calculation and moral rules. Perspectives on Psychological Science, 5(2), 187-202.

Białek, M., De Neys, W. (2017). Dual processes and moral conflict: Evidence for deontological reasoners' intuitive utilitarian sensitivity. Judgment and Decision making, 12(2), 148-167.

Bicchieri, C. (2016). Norms in the wild: How to diagnose, measure, and change social norms. Oxford University Press.

Bina, F. (2024a). Il progresso morale. Il mulino.

Bina, F. (2024b). Normative ethics and agency in progress. Etica & Politica/ Ethics & Politics, XXVI, 3.

Bina, F., (2024c). Limitations of the Ultimatum Game in the study of moral decisions. AJOB Neuroscience, 15(3), 206-208.

Bina, F. (2023). Agency in progress: The ethics, evolution, and psychology of moral change. Doctoral dissertation.

Bina, F. (2022). Models of moral decision-making: Recent advances and normative relevance. Teoria, 42(2), 201-214.

Bina, F., Bonicalzi, S., Croce, M. (2024). Epistemic authorities and skilled agents: A pluralist account of moral expertise. Topoi, 43, 1053-1065.

Bina, F., Canu, E., Guma, F., Reichlin, M., Sibilla, E., Songhorian, S., Tripodi C. (unpublished manuscript). Effects of a moral reasoning intervention on moral justification abilities.

Birch, J. (2021). Toolmaking and the evolution of normative cognition. Biology & Philosophy, 36(1), 4.

Bird, D. W., Bird, R. B., Codding, B. F., Zeanah, D. W. (2019). Variability in the organization and size of hunter-gatherer groups: Foragers do not live in small-scale societies. Journal of Human Evolution, 131, 96-108.

Bloom, P. (2010). How do morals change?. Nature, 464(7288), 490-490.

Boehm, C. (2001). Hierarchy in the forest: The evolution of egalitarian behavior. Harvard University Press.

Boehm, C. (2012). Moral origins: The evolution of virtue, altruism, and shame. Basic Books.

Böhm, R., Rusch, H., Baron, J. (2020). The psychology of intergroup conflict: A review of theories and measures. Journal of Economic Behavior & Organization, 178, 947-962.

Bond, R., Smith, P. B. (1996). Culture and conformity: A meta-analysis of studies using Asch's (1952b, 1956) line judgment task. Psychological Bulletin, 119(1), 111.

Borg, J. S., Hynes, C., Van Horn, J., Grafton, S., Sinnott-Armstrong, W. (2006). Consequences, action, and intention as factors in moral judgments: An fMRI investigation. Journal of Cognitive Neuroscience, 18(5), 803-817.

Boudry, M., Vlerick, M., Edis, T. (2020). The end of science? On human cognitive limitations and how to overcome them. Biology & Philosophy, 35, 1-16.

Bowles, S., Gintis, H. (2013). A cooperative species. Princeton University Press.

Boyd, R., Richerson, P. J. (1992). Punishment allows the evolution of cooperation (or anything else) in sizable groups. Ethology and Sociobiology, 13, 171-195.

Brewer, M. B. (1999). The psychology of prejudice: Ingroup love and outgroup hate?. Journal of Social Issues, 55(3), 429-444.

Brosnan, S. F., de Waal, F. B. M. (2003). Monkeys reject unequal pay. Nature, 425, 297-299.

Brosnan, S. F. (2006). Nonhuman species' reactions to inequity and their implications for fairness. Social Justice Research, 19, 153-185.

Buchanan, A. (2020). Our moral fate: Evolution and the escape from tribalism. MIT Press.

Buchanan, A., Powell, R. (2015). The limits of evolutionary explanations of morality and their implications for moral progress. Ethics, 126(1), 37-67.

Buchanan, A., Powell, R. (2016). Toward a naturalistic theory of moral progress. Ethics, 126(4), 983-1014.

Buchanan, A., Powell, R. (2017). De-moralization as emancipation: Liberty, progress, and the evolution of invalid moral norms. Social Philosophy and Policy, 34(2), 108-135.

Buchanan, A., Powell, R. (2018). The evolution of moral progress: A biocultural theory. Oxford University Press.

Buller, D. J. (1998). Etiological theories of function: A geographical survey. Biology and Philosophy, 13, 505-527.

Buller, D. J. (2005). Adapting minds: Evolutionary psychology and the persistent quest for human nature. MIT Press.

Buss, D. M. (2019). Evolutionary psychology: The new science of the mind. Routledge.

Buss, D. M., Haselton, M. G., Shackelford, T. K., Bleske, A. L., Wakefield, J. C. (1998). Adaptations, exaptations, and spandrels. American Psychologist, 53(5), 533.

Campbell, R. (2017). Learning from moral inconsistency. Cognition, 167, 46-57.

Campbell, R., Kumar, V. (2012). Moral reasoning on the ground. Ethics, 122(2), 273-312.

Campbell, R., Woodrow, J. (2003). Why Moore's open question is open: The evolution of moral supervenience. The Journal of Value Inquiry, 37 (3), 353-372.

Carruthers, P. E., Laurence, S. E., Stich, S. E. (2005). The innate mind: Structure and contents. Oxford University Press.

Casebeer, W. D. (2003). Natural ethical facts: Evolution, connectionism, and moral cognition. MIT Press.

Charities Aid Foundation (2024). World giving index. World trends in generosity.

Chilton, B. D., Neusner, J. (eds.). (2009). The golden rule: The ethics of reciprocity in world religions. Bloomsbury.

Choi, H., Oishi, S. (2020). The psychology of residential mobility: A decade of progress. Current opinion in psychology, 32, 72-75.

Choi, J. K., Bowles, S. (2007). The coevolution of parochial altruism and war. Science, 318(5850), 636-640.

Christensen, M. B, Hallum, C., Maitland, A., Parrinello, Q., Putaturo, C. (2023). Survival of the richest. Oxfam International Briefing Paper.

Chomsky, N. (1975). Reflections on Language. Pantheon Books.

Clark, C. J., Liu, B. S., Winegard, B. M., Ditto, P. H. (2019). Tribalism is human nature. Current Directions in Psychological Science, 28(6), 587-592.

Clark, C. J., Winegard, B. M. (2020). Tribalism in war and peace: The nature and evolution of ideological epistemology and its significance for modern social science. Psychological Inquiry, 31(1), 1-22.

Coleman, J. S. (1990). Foundations of social theory. Harvard University Press.

Confucius. (1994). A single word. In P. Singer (ed.), Ethics. Oxford University Press.

Corr, P. J., Hargreaves Heap, S. P., Seger, C. R., Tsutsui, K. (2015). An experiment on individual 'parochial altruism' revealing no connection between individual 'altruism' and individual 'parochialism'. Frontiers in Psychology, 6, 1261.

Cosmides, L., Tooby, J. (1992). Cognitive adaptations for social exchange. In J. Barkow, L. Cosmides, J. Tooby (eds.), The adapted mind: Evolutionary psychology and the generation of culture. Oxford University Press. 163-228.

Cosmides, L., Tooby, J. (1997). The modular nature of human intelligence. In A. B. Scheibel, J. W. Schopf (eds.). The origin and evolution of intelligence. Jones and Bartlett, 71-101.

Crutchfield, P. (2021). Moral enhancement and the public good. Routledge.

Cummins, D. D. (1996a). Evidence of deontic reasoning in 3- and 4-year-olds. Memory and Cognition, 24, 823-829.

Cummins, D. D. (1996b). Evidence for the innateness of deontic reasoning. Mind & Language, 11, 160-190.

Curry, O. S. (2016). Morality as cooperation: A problem-centred approach. In Shackelford T. K., Hansen, D. (eds.), The evolution of morality. Springer, 25-51.

Curry, O. S., Price, M. E., Price, J. G. (2008). Patience is a virtue: Cooperative people have lower discount rates. Personality and Individual Differences, 44, 778-783.

Cushman, F. (2008). Crime and punishment: Distinguishing the roles of causal and intentional analysis in moral judgment. Cognition, 108(2), 353-380.

Cushman, F. (2013). Action, outcome, and value: A dual-system framework for morality. Personality and Social Psychology Review, 17(3), 273-292.

Cushman, F. (2020). Rationalization is rational. Behavioral and Brain Sciences, 43, e28.

Cushman, F., Gray, K., Gaffey, A., Mendes, W. B. (2012). Simulating murder: the aversion to harmful action. Emotion, 12(1), 2.

Daly, M., Wilson, M. (1988). Homicide. De Gruyter.

Darwin, C. (1872/1998). The expression of the emotions in man and animals (3rd ed.). Harper Collins.

Dawkins, R. (1976). The selfish gene. Oxford University Press.

Dayan, P. (2012). How to set the switches on this thing. Current Opinion in Neurobiology, 22(6), 1068-1074.

De Caro M., Bina F., Vaccarezza M. S., Croce M., Bonicalzi S., Kerusausaite S., Brunetti R., Navarini C. (forthcoming). Virtue monism and medical practice: Practical wisdom as cross-situational ethical expertise. The Journal of Medicine and Philosophy.

De Dreu, C. K., Fariña, A., Gross, J., Romano, A. (2022). Prosociality as a foundation for intergroup conflict. Current Opinion in Psychology, 44, 112-116.

De Neys, W. (2014). Conflict detection, dual processes, and logical intuitions: Some clarifications. Thinking & Reasoning, 20(2), 169-187.

de Waal, F. (2006). Primates and philosophers: How morality evolved. Princeton University Press.

de Waal, F. (1996), Good natured. Harvard University Press.

Dennett, D. C. (2003). Freedom evolves. Penguin.

Dickert, S., Västfjäll, D., Kleber, J., Slovic, P. (2012). Valuations of human lives: normative expectations and psychological mechanisms of (ir) rationality. Synthese, 189(1), 95-105.

Dickinson, A., Balleine, B., Watt, A., Gonzalez, F., Boakes, R. A., (1995). Motivational control after extended instrumental training. Animal Learning & Behavior, 23(2), 197-206.

Dolan, R. J., Dayan, P. (2013). Goals and habits in the brain. Neuron, 80(2), 312-325.

Doris, J. M. (1998). Persons, situations, and virtue ethics. Noûs, 32, 504-530.

Doris, J. M. (2002). Lack of character: Personality and moral behavior. Cambridge University Press.

Douglas, T. (2008). Moral enhancement. Journal of Applied Philosophy, 25(3), 228-245.

Downie, R. S. (1965). Forgiveness. Philosophical Quarterly, 15(59), 128–134.

Dreyfus, H. L., Dreyfus, S. E. (1991). Towards a phenomenology of ethical expertise. Human studies, 229-250.

Dunbar, R. (1993). Coevolution of neocortical size, group size and language in humans. Behavioral and Brain Sciences, 16(4), 681-694.

Dunbar, R. (2004). Gossip in evolutionary perspective. Review of General Psychology, 8(2), 100-110.

Dunbar, R. (2010). How many friends does one person need?. Harvard University Press.

Dworkin, R. (1984). Rights as Trumps. In Waldron J. (ed.). Theories of Rights. Oxford University Press, 153-67.

Dwyer, S., Huebner, B., Hauser, M. D. (2010). The linguistic analogy: Motivations, results, and speculations. Topics in Cognitive Science, 2(3), 486-510.

Edelman, M. S., Omark, D. R. (1973). Dominance hierarchies in young children. Social Science Information, 12(1), 103-110.

Elison, J. (2005). Shame and guilt: A hundred years of apples and oranges. New Ideas in Psychology, 23(1), 5-32.

Emmons, R. A. (ed.). (2004). The psychology of gratitude. Oxford University Press.

Enos, R. D. (2017). The space between us: Social geography and politics. Cambridge University Press.

Ensminger, J., Henrich, J. (eds.). (2014). Experimenting with social norms: Fairness and punishment in cross-cultural perspective. Russell Sage Foundation.

Evans, J. (2017). A working definition of moral Progress. Ethical theory and moral practice, 20, 75-92.

Evans, J. S. B. (2019). Reflections on reflection: the nature and function of type 2 processes in dual-process theories of reasoning. Thinking & Reasoning, 25(4), 383-415.

Evans, J. S. B., Stanovich, K. E. (2013). Dual-process theories of higher cognition: Advancing the debate. Perspectives on Psychological Science, 8(3), 223-241.

Faulkner, J., Schaller, M., Park, J. H., Duncan, L. A. (2004). Evolved disease-avoidance mechanisms and contemporary xenophobic attitudes. Group Processes & Intergroup Relations, 7(4), 333-353.

Fehr, E., Fischbacher, U., Von Rosenbladt, B., Schupp, J., Wagner, G. G. (2002). A nation-wide laboratory: Examining trust and trustworthiness by integrating behavioral experiments into representative survey. CEPR Discussion Papers 122 (141), 519-542.

Fessler, D. (2004). Shame in two cultures: Implications for evolutionary approaches. Journal of Cognition and Culture, 4(2), 207-262.

Festinger, L. (1957). A theory of cognitive dissonance. Stanford University Press.

Fine, C. (2006). Is the emotional dog wagging its rational tail, or chasing it? Reason in moral judgment. Philosophical Explorations, 9(1), 83-98.

FitzPatrick, W. J. (2019). Moral progress for evolved rational creatures. Analyse & Kritik, 41(2), 217-238.

Flanagan, O. J. (1991). Varieties of moral personality: Ethics and psychological realism. Harvard University Press.

Fodor, J. A. (1983). The modularity of mind. MIT Press.

Frankena, W. (1967/1970). The concept of morality. In Wallace, G., Walker, A. D. (1970) (eds.). The definition of morality. Methuen, 146-173.

Fukuyama, F. (1996). Trust: The social virtues and the creation of prosperity. London: Penguin Books.

Fukuyama, F. (2002). Our posthuman future. Farrar, Straus and Giroux.

Gabennesch, H. (1990). The perception of social conventionality by children and adults. Child Development, 61, 2047-2059.

Gallagher, S. (2013). The socially extended mind. Cognitive Systems Research, 25, 4-12.

Garson, J. (2008). Function and teleology. In S. Sarkar, A. Plutynski (eds.). A companion to the philosophy of biology. Blackwell, 525-549.

Gauthier, D. (1987). Morals by agreement. Oxford University Press.

Gert, B., Gert, J. The definition of morality. In E. N. Zalta (ed.). The Stanford Encyclopedia of Philosophy [Online].

Ghiselin, M. (1974). The economy of nature and the evolution of sex. University of California Press.

Gigerenzer, G. (2007). Gut feelings: The intelligence of the unconscious. Penguin.

Gigerenzer, G. E., Hertwig, R. E., Pachur, T. E. (2011). Heuristics: The foundations of adaptive behavior. Oxford University Press.

Gintis, H., Smith, E. A., Bowles, S. (2001). Costly signaling and cooperation. Journal of Theoretical Biology, 213, 103-119.

Godfray, H. C. J. (1992). The evolution of forgiveness. Nature, 355, 206-207.

Godfrey-Smith, P. (1994). A modern history theory of functions. Noûs, 28(3), 344-362.

Goldsmith, J. L., Posner, E. A. (2005). The limits of international law. Oxford University Press.

Goodwin, G. P. (2017). Is morality unified, and does this matter for moral reasoning?. In Bonnefon, J. F., Trémolière, B. (eds.). Moral inferences. Psychology Press, 17-44.

Gould, S. J., Lewontin, R. C. (1979). The spandrels of San Marco and the Panglossian paradigm: a critique of the adaptationist programme. Proceedings of the Royal Society of London B, 205, 581-98.

Gould, S. J., Vrba, E. S. (1982). Exaptation—A missing term in the science of form. Paleobiology, 8(1), 4-15.

Gowdy, J. (1999). Hunter-gatherers and the mythology of the market. In Lee, R. B., Daly, R. H., Daly, R. (eds.). The Cambridge encyclopedia of hunters and gatherers. Cambridge University Press, 391-398.

Granovetter, M. S. (1973). The strength of weak ties. American Journal of Sociology, 78(6), 1360-1380.

Gray, K., Wegner, D. M. (2009). Moral typecasting: Divergent perceptions of moral agent and moral patients. Journal of Personality and Social Psychology, 96(3), 505-520.

Graybiel, A. M. (2008). Habits, rituals, and the evaluative brain. Annual Review of Neuroscience, 31, 359-387.

Greene, J. D. (2003). From neural 'is' to moral 'ought': What are the moral implications of neuroscientific moral psychology?. Nature Reviews Neuroscience, 4(10), 846-850.

Greene, J. D. (2007). The secret joke of Kant's soul. In W. Sinnott-Armstrong (ed.), Moral psychology: The neuroscience of morality: Emotion, disease, and development (Vol. 3). MIT Press, 35-79.

Greene, J. D. (2013). Moral tribes: Emotion, reason, and the gap between us and them. Penguin.

Greene, J. D. (2014). Beyond point-and-shoot morality: Why cognitive (neuro) science matters for ethics. Ethics, 124(4), 695-726.

Greene, J. D. (2015). The rise of moral cognition. Cognition, 135, 39-42.

Greene, J. D. (2017). The rat-a-gorical imperative: Moral intuition and the limits of affective learning. Cognition, 167, 66-77.

Greene, J. D. (forthcoming). Dual-process moral judgement beyond fast and slow. Behavioral and Brain Sciences.

Greene, J. D., Sommerville, R. B., Nystrom, L. E., Darley, J. M., Cohen, J. D. (2001). An fMRI investigation of emotional engagement in moral judgment. Science, 293(5537), 2105-2108.

Greene, J. D., Nystrom, L. E., Engell, A. D., Darley, J. M., Cohen, J. D. (2004). The neural bases of cognitive conflict and control in moral judgment. Neuron, 44, 389-400.

Greene, J. D., Cushman, F. A., Stewart, L. E., Lowenberg, K., Nystrom, L. E., Cohen, J. D. (2009). Pushing moral buttons: The interaction between personal force and intention in moral judgment. Cognition, 111(3), 364-371.

Greene, J. D., Young, L. (2020). The cognitive neuroscience of moral judgment and decision-making. In M.S. Gazzaniga (ed.). The Cognitive Neuroscience, Volume 6. MIT Press.

Griffiths, P. E., Machery, E., Linquist, S. (2009). The vernacular concept of innateness. Mind & Language, 24, 605-630.

Guardo, A. (2024). L'evoluzione della morale per selezione naturale. Raffaello Cortina.

Gürçay, B., Baron J. (2017). Challenges for the sequential two-system model of moral judgement. Thinking & Reasoning, 23(1), 49-80.

Gurven, M., Von Rueden, C., Massenkoff, M., Kaplan, H., Lero Vie, M. (2013). How universal is the Big Five? Testing the five-factor model of personality variation among forager–farmers in the Bolivian Amazon. Journal of Personality and Social Psychology, 104(2), 354.

Güth, W., Schmittberger, R., Schwarze, B. (1982). An experimental analysis of ultimatum bargaining. Journal of Economic Behavior & Organization, 3(4), 367-388.

Haerpfer, C., Inglehart, R., Moreno, A., Welzel, C., Kizilova, K., Diez-Medrano J., M. Lagos, P. Norris, E. Ponarin & B. Puranen et al. (eds.) (2022). World Values Survey Trend File (1981-2022) Cross-National Data-Set.

Hadot, P. (1995). Philosophy as a way of life. Blackwell.

Haidt, J. (2001). The emotional dog and its rational tail: A social intuitionist approach to moral judgment. Psychological Review, 108(4), 814-834.

Haidt, J. (2012). The righteous mind: Why good people are divided by politics and religion. Pantheon Books.

Haidt, J., Koller, S. H., Dias, M. G. (1993). Affect, culture, and morality, or is it wrong to eat your dog?. Journal of Personality and Social Psychology, 65(4), 613.

Han, H. (2017). Neural correlates of moral sensitivity and moral judgment associated with brain circuitries of selfhood: A meta-analysis. Journal of Moral Education, 46(2), 97-113.

Hardin, G. J. (1977). The limits of altruism: An ecologist's view of survival. Bloomington.

Hardy, C. L., Van Vugt, M. (2006). Nice guys finish first: The competitive altruism hypothesis. Personality and Social Psychology Bulletin, 32(10), 1402-1413.

Hardy, C. W., Briffa, M. (eds.). (2013). Animal contests. Cambridge University Press.

Harris, J. (2011). Moral enhancement and freedom. Bioethics, 25(2), 102-11.

Harris, J. (2012). What it's like to be good. Cambridge Quarterly of Healthcare Ethics, 21(3), 293-305.

Harris, J. (2016). How to be good: The possibility of moral enhancement. Oxford University Press.

Harris, P. L., Nuñez M. (1996). Understanding of permission rules by preschool children. Child Development, 67, 1572-1591.

Haselton, M. G., Nettle, D. (2006). The paranoid optimist: An integrative evolutionary model of cognitive biases. Personality and Social Psychology Review, 10(1), 47-66.

Hauser, M. D. (2006). Moral minds: How nature designed our universal sense of right and wrong. Ecco.

Henrich, J. (2000). Does culture matter in economic behavior? Ultimatum game bargaining among the Machiguenga of the Peruvian Amazon. American Economic Review, 90(4), 973-979.

Henrich, J. (2015). The secret of our success. Princeton University Press.

Henrich, J. (2020). The WEIRDest people in the world: How the West became psychologically peculiar and particularly prosperous. Penguin.

Henrich, J., Boyd, R., Bowles, S., Camerer, C., Fehr, E., Gintis, H., McElreath, R. (2001). In search of homo economicus: behavioral experiments in 15 small-scale societies. American Economic Review, 91(2), 73-78.

Henrich, J., Boyd, R., Fehr, E., Bowles, S., Camerer, C., Gintis, H. (eds.). (2004). Foundations of human sociality: Economic experiments and ethnographic evidence from fifteen small-scale societies. Oxford University Press.

Henrich, J., Boyd, R., Bowles, S., Camerer, C., Fehr, E., Gintis, H., et al. (2005). 'Economic Man' in cross-cultural perspective: Behavioral experiments in 15 small-scale societies. Behavioral and Brain Sciences, 28(6), 795-855.

Henrich, J., Heine, S. J., Norenzayan, A. (2010). Most people are not WEIRD. Nature, 466(7302), 29-29.

Hickman, C., Marks, E., Pihkala, P., Clayton, S., Lewandowski, R. E., Mayall, E. E., Wray, B., Mellor, C., Van Susteren, L. (2021). Climate anxiety in children and young people and their beliefs about government responses to climate change: a global survey. The Lancet Planetary Health, 5(12), e863-e873.

Hindriks, F., Sauer, H. (2020). The mark of the moral: Beyond the sentimentalist turn. Philosophical Psychology, 33(4), 569-591.

Hobbes, T. (1651/1958). Leviathan. Macmillan.

Hofstede, G. H. (2003). Culture's consequences: Comparing values, behaviors, institutions and organizations across nations (2nd ed.). Sage.

Hopster, J. (2020). Explaining historical moral convergence: the empirical case against realist intuitionism. Philosophical Studies, 177(5), 1255-1273.

Huemer, M. (2016). A liberal realist answer to debunking skeptics: the empirical case for realism. Philosophical Studies, 173, 1983-2010.

Huemer, M. (2019). Dialogues on ethical vegetarianism. Routledge.

Huxley, H. (1893/2009), Evolution and Ethics. Princeton University Press.

Inglehart, R. F. (2018). Cultural evolution: People's motivations are changing, and reshaping the world. Cambridge University Press.

Ipsos (2024), Global attitudes towards women's leadership.

Ipsos, UNHCR (2024), Global attutudes toward refugees.

Ivanhoe, P. J. (2000). Confucian moral self-cultivation. Hackett.

Jamieson, D. (2002). Is there progress in morality?. Utilitas, 14(3), 318-338.

Jebari, K. (2014). What to enhance: Behaviour, emotion or disposition?. Neuroethics, 7(3), 253-261.

Johnson, N. D., Mislin, A. A. (2011). Trust games: A meta-analysis. Journal of economic psychology, 32(5), 865-889.

Joyce, R. (2006). The evolution of morality. MIT Press.

Jost, J. T., Glaser, J., Kruglanski, A. W., Sulloway, F. J., (2003). Political conservatism as motivated social cognition. Psychological Bulletin, 3, 339-375.

Kahane, G., Wiech, K., Shackel, N., Farias, M., Savulescu, J., Tracey, I. (2012). The neural basis of intuitive and counterintuitive moral judgment. Social Cognitive and Affective Neuroscience, 7(4), 393-402.

Kahneman, D. (2003). A perspective on judgment and choice: Mapping bounded rationality. American Psychologist, 58(9), 697-720.

Kahneman, D. (2011). Thinking, fast and slow. Macmillan.

Kant, I. (1785/1996). Groundwork for the metaphysics of morals. Cambridge University Press.

Kelly, D., Stich, S., Haley, K. J., Eng, S. J., Fessler, D. M. (2007). Harm, affect, and the moral/conventional distinction. Mind & Language, 22(2), 117-131.

Kennett, J., Matthews, S. (2009). Mental timetravel, agency and responsibility. In M. Broome L. Bortolotti (eds.), Psychiatry as cognitive neuroscience: Philosophical perspectives. Oxford University Press, 327-350.

Keramati, M., Dezfouli, A., Piray P. (2011). Speed/accuracy trade-off between the habitual and the goal-directed processes. PLoS Computational Biology, 7(5), e1002055.

Kitcher, P. (1993). Function and design. Midwest Studies in Philosophy, 18, 379-397.

Kitcher, P. (2005). Biology and ethics. In D. Copp (ed.), The Oxford handbook of ethical theory. Oxford University Press, 163-185.

Kitcher, P. (2011). The ethical project. Harvard University Press.

Kitcher, P. (2017). Social progress. Social Philosophy and Policy, 34(2), 46-65.

Kitcher, P. (2021). Moral progress. Oxford University Press.

Klenk, M., Sauer, H. (2021). Moral judgement and moral progress: The problem of cognitive control. Philosophical Psychology, 34(7), 938–961.

Knafo, A., Schwartz, S. H., Levine, R. V. (2009). Helping strangers is lower in embedded cultures. Journal of Cross-Cultural Psychology, 40(5), 875-879.

Kohlberg, L. (1981, 1984). Essays on moral development (Volumes I and II). Harper & Row.

Kool, W., Gershman, S. J., Cushman, F. A. (2017). Cost-benefit arbitration between multiple reinforcement-learning systems. Psychological Science, 28(9), 1321-1333.

Kool, W., Cushman, F. A., Gershman, S. J. (2018). Competition and cooperation between multiple reinforcement learning systems. In Morris, R. W., Bornstein, A., Shenhav, A. (eds.). Goal-directed decision making: Computations and neural circuits. Academic Press, 153-178.

Koop, G. J. (2013). An assessment of the temporal dynamics of moral decisions. Judgment and Decision Making, 8(5), 527.

Korsgaard, C. M. (2006). Morality and the distinctiveness of human action. In F. de Waal (2006). Primates and philosophers. Princeton University Press.

Krebs, D. (2011). The origins of morality: An evolutionary account. Oxford University Press.

Kristjánsson, K. (2007). Aristotle, emotions, and education. Routledge.

Kristjánsson, K. (2015). Aristotelian character education. Routledge.

Kumar, V., Campbell, R. (2022). A better ape: The evolution of the moral mind and how it made us human, Oxford University Press.

Kumar, V., Kodipady, A., Young, L. (2023). A psychological account of the unique decline in anti-gay attitudes. Philosophical Psychology, 1-35.

Kunda, Z. (1990). The case for motivated reasoning. Psychological Bulletin, 108(3), 480-498.

Kurzban, R., Leary, M. R. (2001). Evolutionary origins of stigmatization: The functions of social exclusion. Psychological Bulletin, 127(2), 187.

Lee, W. E. (2016). Waging war: Conflict, culture, and innovation in world history. Oxford University Press.

Levy, N. (2021). Bad beliefs: Why they happen to good people. Oxford University Press.

Li, N. P., van Vugt, M., Colarelli, S. M. (2018). The evolutionary mismatch hypothesis: Implications for psychological science. Current Directions in Psychological Science, 27(1), 38-44.

Lickliter, R., Honeycutt, H. (2003). Developmental dynamics: toward a biologically plausible evolutionary psychology. Psychological Bulletin, 129(6), 819.

Luco, A. (2014). The definition of morality: Threading the needle. Social Theory and Practice, 361-387.

Luco, A. (2019). How moral facts cause moral progress. Journal of the American Philosophical Association, 5(4), 429-448.

Lun, J., Oishi, S., Tenney, E. R. (2012). Residential mobility moderates preferences for egalitarian versus loyal helpers. Journal of Experimental Social Psychology, 48(1), 291-297.

Ma, V., Schoeneman, T. J. (1997). Individualism versus collectivism: A comparison of Kenyan and American self-concepts. Basic and applied social psychology, 19(2), 261-273.

Machery, E., Mallon, R. (2010). Evolution of morality. Doris, J. M., & Moral Psychology Research Group. The Moral Psychology Handbook. Oxford University Press.

Machery, E., Stich, E. (2022). The moral/conventional distinction. In E. N Zalta (ed.). The Stanford Encyclopedia of Philosophy [Online].

Macklin, R. (1977). Moral progress. Ethics, 87(4), 370-382.

Madva, A. (2016). A plea for anti-anti-individualism: How oversimple psychology misleads social policy. Ergo, 3, 27, 701-728.

Mallon, R., Weinberg, J. (2006). Innateness as closed-process invariantism. Philosophy of Science, 73, 323-344.

Marlowe, F. W., Berbesque, J. C., Barr, A., Barrett, C., Bolyanatz, A., Cardenas, J. C., Ensminger, G., Gurven, M., Gwako, E., Henrich, J., Henrich, N., Lesogorol, C., McElreath, R., Tracer, D. (2008). More 'altruistic' punishment in larger societies. Proceedings of the Royal Society B: Biological Sciences, 275(1634), 587-592.

Mathieu, E., Ritchie, H. (2022). What share of people say they are vegetarian, vegan, or flexitarian?. Our World in Data (online).

May, J. (2013). Because I believe it's the right thing to do. Ethical Theory and Moral Practice, 16, 791-808.

Maynard Smith, J. (1982). Evolution and the theory of games. Cambridge University Press.

Maynard Smith, J., Price, G. R. (1973). The logic of animal conflict. Nature, 246, 15-18.

McCloskey, D. N. (2010). The bourgeois virtues: Ethics for an age of commerce. University of Chicago Press.

McDonald, M. M., Navarrete, C. D., Van Vugt, M. (2012). Evolution and the psychology of intergroup conflict: The male warrior hypothesis. Philosophical Transactions of the Royal Society B: Biological Sciences, 367(1589), 670-679.

McNamara, R. A., Willard, A. K., Norenzayan, A., Henrich, J. (2019). Weighing outcome vs. intent across societies: How cultural models of mind shape moral reasoning. Cognition, 182, 95-108.

Mercier, H., Sperber, D. (2017). The enigma of reason. Harvard University Press.

Mikhail, J. (2007). Universal moral grammar: Theory, evidence and the future. Trends in Cognitive Sciences, 11(4), 143-152.

Mill, J. S. (1859/2003). On liberty. In M. Warnock (ed.). Utilitarianism and on liberty (2nd ed.). Blackwell.

Millikan, R. G. (1984). Language, thought and other biological categories. MIT Press.

Millikan, R. G. (1989). In defense of proper functions. Philosophy of Science, 56(2), 288-302.

Moody-Adams, M. M. (2017). Moral progress and human agency. Ethical Theory and Moral Practice, 20(1), 153-168.

Moody-Adams, M. M. (1999). The idea of moral progress. Metaphilosophy, 30(3), 168-185.

Musschenga, A. W., Meynen, G. (2017). Moral progress: An introduction. Ethical Theory and Moral Practice, 20, 3-15.

Muthukrishna, M., Henrich, J., Slingerland, E. (2021). Psychology as a historical science. Annual Review of Psychology, 72, 717-749.

Nagel, T. (2012). Mind and cosmos: Why the materialist neo-Darwinian conception of nature is almost certainly false. Oxford University Press.

Nash, J. (1950). The bargaining problem. Econometrica, 18, 155-162.

Navarrete, C. D., Fessler, D. M. (2006). Disease avoidance and ethnocentrism: The effects of disease vulnerability and disgust sensitivity on intergroup attitudes. Evolution and Human Behavior, 27(4), 270-282.

Neander, K. (1991). The teleological notion of 'function'. Australasian Journal of Philosophy, 69(4), 454-468.

Neuberg, S. L., Schaller, M. (2016). An evolutionary threat-management approach to prejudices. Current Opinion in Psychology, 7, 1-5.

Nichols, S. (2004). Sentimental rules: On the natural foundations of moral judgment. Oxford University Press.

Norenzayan, A., Shariff, A. F., Gervais, W. M., Willard, A. K., McNamara, R. A., Slingerland, E., Henrich, J. (2016). The cultural evolution of prosocial religions. Behavioral and brain sciences, 39, e1.

Nowak, M, Sigmund, K. (2005). Evolution of indirect reciprocity. Nature, 437, 1291-1298

Oaten, M., Stevenson, R. J., Case, T. I. (2011). Disease avoidance as a functional basis for stigmatization. Philosophical Transactions of the Royal Society B: Biological Sciences, 366(1583), 3433-3452.

Ohtsubo, Y., Watanabe, E. (2009). Do sincere apologies need to be costly? Test of a costly signaling model of apology. Evolution and Human Behavior, 30(2), 114-123.

Page, L. (2022). Optimally irrational: The good reasons we behave the way we do. Cambridge University Press.

Parkinson, C., Sinnott-Armstrong, W., Koralus, P. E., Mendelovici, A., McGeer, V., Wheatley, T. (2011). Is morality unified? Evidence that distinct neural systems underlie moral judgments of harm, dishonesty, and disgust. Journal of Cognitive Neuroscience, 23(10), 3162-3180.

Pascual, L., Gallardo-Pujol, D., Rodrigues, P. (2013). How does morality work in the brain? A functional and structural perspective of moral behavior. Frontiers in Integrative Neuroscience, 7(65), 1-8.

Paxton, J. M., Ungar, L., Greene, J. D. (2012). Reflection and reasoning in moral judgment. Cognitive science, 36(1), 163-177.

Persson, I., Savulescu, J. (2008). The perils of cognitive enhancement and the urgent imperative to enhance the moral character of humanity. Journal of Applied Philosophy, 25(3), 162-177.

Persson, I., Savulescu, J. (2012). Unfit for the future: The need for moral enhancement. Oxford University Press.

Persson, I., Savulescu, J. (2017). Moral hard wiring and moral enhancement. Bioethics, 31(4), 286-295.

Phillips, J., Cushman, F. (2017). Morality constrains the default representation of what is possible. Proceedings of the National Academy of Sciences, 114(18), 4649-4654.

Pietraszewski, D, Wertz, A. E. (2022). Why evolutionary psychology should abandon modularity. Perspectives on Psychological Science, 17(2), 465-490.

Pinker, S. (1997). How the mind works. Norton.

Pinker, S. (2002). The blank slate: The modern denial of human nature. Penguin.

Pinker, S. (2011). The better angels of our nature: The decline of violence in history and its causes. Penguin.

Pinker, S. (2018). Enlightenment now: The case for reason, science, humanism, and progress. Penguin.

Pisor A. C., Surbeck M. (2019). The evolution of intergroup tolerance in nonhuman primates and humans. Evolutionary Anthropology 28(4), 210-223.

Powell, R., Buchanan, A. (2016). The Evolution of Moral Enhancement. In S. Clarke, J. Savulescu (eds.). The ethics of human enhancement: Understanding the debate. Oxford University Press, 239-260.

Preuschoft, S., van Schaik, C. P. (2000). Dominance and communication: Conflict management in various social settings. In F. Aureli, F. de Waal (eds.), Natural conflict resolution (77-105). University of California Press.

Prinz, J. (2006a). The emotional basis of moral judgments. Philosophical Explorations, 9(1), 29-43.

Prinz, J. (2006b). Is the mind really modular?. Contemporary Debates in Cognitive Science, 14, 22-36.

Prinz, J. (2007). The emotional construction of morals. Oxford University Press.

Prinz, J. (2008). Is morality innate?. In Sinnott-Armstrong, W. E. (ed.). Moral psychology, Vol 1. The evolution of morality: Adaptations and innateness. MIT Press, 367-406.

Prinz, J. (2012). Beyond human nature: How culture and experience shape the human mind. Norton.

Rai, T. S., Fiske, A. P. (2011). Moral psychology is relationship regulation: moral motives for unity, hierarchy, equality, and proportionality. Psychological review, 118(1), 57.

Railton, P. (2014). The affective dog and its rational tale: Intuition and attunement. Ethics, 124(4), 813-859.

Railton, P. (2017). Moral learning: Conceptual foundations and normative relevance. Cognition, 167, 172-190.

Rand, D. G., Greene, J. D., Nowak, M. A. (2012). Spontaneous giving and calculated greed. Nature, 489(7416), 427-430.

Rand, D. G., Peysakhovich, A., Kraft-Todd, G. T., Newman, G. E., Wurzbacher, O., Nowak, M. A., Greene, J. D. (2014). Social heuristics shape intuitive cooperation. Nature communications, 5(1), 3677.

Rawls, J. (1951). Outline of a decision procedure for ethics. The Philosophical Review, 60(2), 177-197.

Rawls, J. (1971). A Theory of Justice. Harvard University Press.

Rebonato, R. (2012). Taking liberties: A critical examination of libertarian paternalism. Springer.

Reger, J., Lind, M. I., Robinson, M. R., Beckerman, A. P. (2018). Predation drives local adaptation of phenotypic plasticity. Nature Ecology & Evolution, 2(1), 100-107.

Reichlin, M. (2019). The moral agency argument against moral bioenhancement. Topoi, 38(1), 53-62.

Rhoads, S. A., Gunter, D., Ryan, R. M., Marsh, A. A. (2021). Global variation in subjective well-being predicts seven forms of altruism. Psychological Science, 32(8), 1247-1261.

Richards, N. (1988). Forgiveness. Ethics, 99(1), 77-97.

Richerson, P. J., Boyd, R. (1999). Complex societies: The evolutionary origins of a crude superorganism. Human nature, 10, 253-289.

Riechert, S. E. (1998). Game theory and animal contests. In L. A. Dugatkin H. K. Reeve (Eds.), Game theory and animal behavior (64-93). Oxford University Press.

Ritchie, H., Rosado, P., Roser, M. (2017). Meat and dairy production. Our World in Data.

Rorty R. (1999). Human rights, rationality and sentimentality. In O. Savic (ed.). The politics of human rights. Verso, 67-83.

Ross, D. (2018). The elephant as a person. Aeon, 24 October.

Runge, C. F. (1984). Institutions and the free rider: The assurance problem in collective action. The Journal of Politics, 46(1), 154-181.

Ruse, M. (2009). Philosophy after Darwin. Princeton University Press.

Rustagi, D., Engel, S., Kosfeld, M. (2010). Conditional cooperation and costly monitoring explain success in forest commons management. Science, *330*(6006), 961-965.

Samuels, R. (1998). Evolutionary psychology and the massive modularity hypothesis. British Journal for the Philosophy of Science, 49, 575-602.

Samuels, R. (2002). Nativism in cognitive science. Mind & Language, 17, 233-265.

Santos, H. C., Varnum, M. E., Grossmann, I. (2017). Global increases in individualism. Psychological Science, 28(9), 1228-1239.

Sauer, H. (2012). Educated intuitions. Automaticity and rationality in moral judgement. Philosophical Explorations, 15(3), 255-275.

Sauer, H. (2017). Moral judgments as educated intuitions. MIT Press.

Sauer, H. (2019). Butchering benevolence moral progress beyond the expanding circle. Ethical Theory and Moral Practice, 22(1), 153-167.

Sauer, H. (2023). Moral teleology: A theory of progress. Routledge.

Savulescu, J., Persson, I. (2012). Moral enhancement, freedom and the god machine. The Monist, 95(3), 399-42.

Scanlon, T. (1998). What we owe to each other. Harvard University Press.

Schaefer, G. O., Savulescu, J. (2019). Procedural moral enhancement. Neuroethics, 12(1), 73-84.

Schulz, A. W. (2020). Enhancing thoughts: Culture, technology, and the evolution of human cognitive uniqueness. Mind & Language, 37(3), 465-484.

Schulz, J. F. (2022). Kin networks and institutional development. The Economic Journal, 132(647), 2578-2613.

Schulz, J. F., Bahrami-Rad, D., Beauchamp, J. P., Henrich, J. (2019). The Church, intensive kinship, and global psychological variation. Science, 366(6466), eaau5141.

Schwitzgebel, E., Cushman, F. (2015). Philosophers' biased judgments persist despite training, expertise and reflection. Cognition, 141, 127-137.

Schwitzgebel, E., Rust, J. (2016). The behavior of ethicists. In Sytsma, J., Buckwalter, W. (eds.) (2016). A companion to experimental philosophy. Wiley, 225-233.

Schwitzgebel, E., Cokelet, B., Singer, P. (2020). Do ethics classes influence student behavior? Case study: Teaching the ethics of eating meat. Cognition, 203, 104397.

Schwitzgebel, E., Cokelet, B., Singer, P. (2023). Students eat less meat after studying meat ethics. Review of philosophy and psychology, 14(1), 113-138.

Segovia-Cuéllar, A., Del Savio, L. (2021). On the use of evolutionary mismatch theories in debating human prosociality. Medicine, Health Care and Philosophy, 24(3), 305-314.

Severini, E. (2021). Moral progress and evolution: Knowledge versus understanding. Ethical Theory and Moral Practice, 24(1), 87-105.

Shafer-Landau, R. (2012). Evolutionary debunking, moral realism and moral knowledge. Journal of Ethics and Social Philosophy, 7, 1, 1-37.

Shariff, A. F., Norenzayan, A. (2007). God is watching you: Priming God concepts increases prosocial behavior in an anonymous economic game. Psychological science, 18(9), 803-809.

Shariff, A. F., Norenzayan, A. (2011). Mean gods make good people: Different views of God predict cheating behavior. The International Journal for the Psychology of Religion, 21(2), 85-96.

Shenhav, A., Greene, J. D. (2010). Moral judgments recruit domain-general valuation mechanisms to integrate representations of probability and magnitude. Neuron, 67(4), 667-677.

Shweder, R. A., Mahapatra, M., Miller, J. (1987). Culture and moral development. In J. Kagan, S. Lamb (eds.), The emergence of morality in young children. University of Chicago Press, 1-82.

Sinclair, N. (2012). Metaethics, teleosemantics and the function of moral judgments. Biology and Philosophy, 27(5), 639-662.

Singer, P. (2023). The meat paradox. The Atlantic, May 24.

Singer, P. (1981/2011). The expanding circle: Ethics, evolution, and moral progress. Princeton University Press.

Singer, P. (2005). Ethics and intuitions. The Journal of Ethics, 9(3/4), 331-352.

Singer, P., Wells, D. (1984). The reproduction revolution: New ways of making babies. Oxford University Press.

Sinnott-Armstrong, W., Wheatley, T. (2014). Are moral judgments unified?. Philosophical Psychology, 27(4), 451-474.

Skyrms, B. (1996). Evolution of the social contract. Cambridge University Press

Slote, M. (2007). The ethics of care and empathy. Routledge.

Smaldino, P. E., Lukaszewski, A., von Rueden, C., Gurven, M. (2019). Niche diversity can explain cross-cultural differences in personality structure. Nature Human Behaviour, 3(12), 1276-1283.

Smetana, J. (1981). Preschool children's conceptions of moral and social rules. Child Development, 52, 1333-1336.

Smith, A. (1759/2004). The theory of moral sentiments. Cambridge University Press.

Smyth, N. (2017). The function of morality. Philosophical Studies, 174(5), 1127-1144.

Smyth, N. (2020). A genealogy of emancipatory values. Inquiry, 1-30.

Songhorian, S. (2019). The methods of neuroethics: Is the neuroscience of ethics really a new challenge to moral philosophy?. Rivista internazionale di Filosofia e Psicologia, 10(1), 1-15.

Songhorian, S., Guma, F., Bina, F., Reichlin, M. (2022). Moral progress: *Just* a matter of behavior?, Teoria, 42(2), 175-187.

Sperber, D. (1996). Explaining culture: A naturalistic approach. Blackwell.

Stanford, P. K. (2018). The difference between ice cream and Nazis: Moral externalization and the evolution of human cooperation. Behavioral and Brain Sciences, 41, 1-49.

Stehr, N. (2006). The moralization of the markets. Routledge.

Sterelny, K. (2010). Moral nativism: A sceptical response. Mind & Language, 25(3), 279-297.

Sterelny, K. (2012). The evolved apprentice. MIT press.

Sterelny, K. (2019). Evolutionary foundations for a theory of moral progress?. Analyse & Kritik, 41(2), 205-216.

Stich, S. (2019). The quest for the boundaries of morality. In A. Zimmerman, K. Jones, M. Timmons (eds.), The Routledge handbook of moral epistemology. Routledge, 15-37.

Stoks, R., Govaert, L., Pauwels, K., Jansen, B., De Meester, L. (2016). Resurrecting complexity: The interplay of plasticity and rapid evolution in the multiple trait response to strong changes in predation pressure in the water flea *Daphnia magna*. Ecology Letters, 19(2), 180-190.

Stotz, K. (2014). Extended evolutionary psychology: the importance of transgenerational developmental plasticity. Frontiers in Psychology, 5, 908.

Street, S. (2006). A Darwinian dilemma for realist theories of value. Philosophical Studies, 127, 109-166.

Sunstein, C. R. (2005). Moral heuristics. Behavioral and brain sciences, 28(4), 531-541.

Symons D. (1992). On the use and misuse of Darwinism in the study of human behavior. In Barkow J., Cosmides L., Tooby J. (eds.), The adapted mind: Evolutionary psychology and the generation of culture. Oxford University Press, 137-159.

Tam, A. (2020). Why moral reasoning is insufficient for moral progress. Journal of Political Philosophy, 28(1), 73-96.

Thaler, R. H., Sunstein, C. R. (2008). Nudge: Improving decisions about health, wealth, and happiness. Penguin.

Thompson, V. A., Turner, J. A. P., Pennycook, G. (2011). Intuition, reason, and metacognition. Cognitive psychology, 63(3), 107-140.

Tomasello, M. (2018). Precís of a natural history of human morality. Philosophical Psychology, 31(5), 661-668.

Tomasello, M. (2016). A natural history of human morality. Harvard University Press.

Tomasello, M., Vaish, A. (2013). Origins of human cooperation and morality. Annual Review of Psychology, 64, 231-255.

Tooby, J. (2020). Evolutionary psychology as the crystalizing core of a unified modern social science. Evolutionary Behavioral Sciences, 14(4), 390-403.

Tooby, J., Cosmides, L. (1990). On the universality of human nature and the uniqueness of the individual: The role of genetics and adaptation. Journal of Personality, 58(1), 17-67.

Triandis, H. C. (1995). Individualism and collectivism. Westview Press.

Tosi, J., Warmke, B. (2016). Moral grandstanding. Philosophy & Public Affairs, 44(3), 197-217.

Tosi, J., Warmke, B. (2020a). Moral grandstanding as a threat to free expression. Social Philosophy and Policy, 37(2), 170-189.

Tosi, J., Warmke, B. (2020b). Grandstanding: The use and abuse of moral talk. Oxford University Press.

Trivers, R. L. (1971). The evolution of reciprocal altruism. The Quarterly review of biology, 46(1), 35-57.

Tropp, L. (ed.). (2012). The Oxford handbook of intergroup conflict. Oxford University Press.

Turiel, E. (1983). The development of social knowledge. Cambridge University Press.

Uchiyama, R., Spicer, R., Muthukrishna, M. (2022). Cultural evolution of genetic heritability. Behavioral and Brain Sciences, 45, e152.

Wallbott, H. G., Scherer, K. R. (1995). Cultural determinants in experiencing shame and guilt. Guilford Press.

Watkins, A. (2021). Testing for phenotypic plasticity. Philosophy, Theory, and Practice in Biology, 13, 3.

Waytz, A., Gray, K., Epley, N., Wegner, D. M. (2010). Causes and consequences of mind perception. Trends in Cognitive Sciences, 14(8), 383-388.

Welzel, C. (2007). Are levels of democracy affected by mass attitudes? Testing attainment and sustainment effects on democracy. International Political Science Review, 28(4), 397-424.

Welzel, C. (2013). Freedom rising. Cambridge University Press.

Welzel, C., Inglehart, R. (2010). Agency, values, and well-being: A human development model. Social Indicators Research, 97, 43-63.

Wilson, E.O. (1975). Sociobiology: The new synthesis. Harvard University Press.

Wisneski, D. C., Skitka, L. J., Morgan, G. S. (2011). Political moralization in the 2012 election. In Proposal for questions on the 2012 Evaluations of Government and Society Survey.

World Bank (2024). Women, Business and the Law.

Wrangham, R. (2009). Catching fire: How cooking made us human. Basic Books.

Wrangham, R. W., Peterson, D. (1996). Demonic males: Apes and the origins of human violence. Houghton Mifflin Harcourt.

Wright, J. C., Warren, M. T., Snow, N. E. (2020). Understanding virtue: Theory and measurement. Oxford University Press.

Wright, L. (1976). Teleological explanations: An etiological analysis of goals and functions. University of California Press.

Yamagishi, T., Mifune, N. (2016). Parochial altruism: Does it explain modern human group psychology?. Current Opinion in Psychology, 7, 39-43.

Young, L., Dungan, J. (2012). Where in the brain is morality? Everywhere and maybe nowhere. Social neuroscience, 7(1), 1-10.

Zagzebski, L. T. (2017). Exemplarist moral theory. Oxford University Press.

Zmigrod, L. (2022). A psychology of ideology: Unpacking the psychological structure of ideological thinking. Perspectives on Psychological Science, 17(4), 1072-1092.

Zmigrod, L., Eisenberg, I. W., Bissett, P. G., Robbins, T. W., Poldrack, R. A. (2021). The cognitive and perceptual correlates of ideological attitudes: a data-driven approach. Philosophical Transactions of the Royal Society B, 376(1822), 20200424.

Printed by
Rotomail Italia S.p.A.
June 2025